BLUE-COLLAR BLUES:
Is Trade to Blame
for Rising US
Income Inequality?

BLUE-COLLAR BLUES:
Is Trade to Blame
for Rising US
Income Inequality?

Robert Z. Lawrence

PETERSON INSTITUTE FOR INTERNATIONAL ECONOMICS
Washington, DC
January 2008

Robert Z. Lawrence has been a nonresident senior fellow at the Peterson Institute since 2001. He is the Albert L. Williams Professor of Trade and Investment at the John F. Kennedy School of Government at Harvard University. He was appointed by President Clinton to serve as a member of his Council of Economic Advisers in 1999. He held the New Century Chair as a nonresident senior fellow at the Brookings Institution and founded and edited the *Brookings Trade Forum*.

He was a senior fellow in the Economic Studies Program at Brookings (1983–91), a professorial lecturer at the Johns Hopkins School of Advanced International Studies (1978–81), and an instructor at Yale University (1975). He served as a consultant to the Federal Reserve Bank of New York, the World Bank, the Organization for Economic Cooperation and Development, and UN Conference on Trade and Development.

He is author or coauthor of several books, including *A US-Middle East Trade Agreement: A Circle of Opportunity?* (2006), *Case Studies in US Trade Negotiation* (2006), *Anchoring Reform with a US-Egypt Free Trade Agreement* (2005), *Has Globalization Gone Far Enough? The Costs of Fragmented Markets* (2004), *Crimes and Punishment? Retaliation under the WTO* (2003), and *Globaphobia: Confronting Fears about Open Trade* (1998).

PETER G. PETERSON INSTITUTE FOR INTERNATIONAL ECONOMICS
1750 Massachusetts Avenue, NW
Washington, DC 20036-1903
(202) 328-9000   FAX: (202) 659-3225
www.petersoninstitute.org

C. Fred Bergsten, *Director*
Edward Tureen, *Director of Publications Marketing, and Web Development*

Copyediting by Madona Devasahayam
Typesetting by BMWW
Printing by Kirby Lithographic Company, Inc.

Printed in the United States of America
10 09 08   5 4 3 2 1

Library of Congress Cataloging-in-Publication Data

Lawrence, Robert Z., 1949–
   Blue-collar blues : is trade to blame for rising US income inequality? / Robert Z. Lawrence
      p. cm.
   Includes bibliographical references and index.
      ISBN 978-0-88132-414-3 (alk. paper)
      1. Income distribution—United States. 2. Wages—United States.   3. United States—Commerce.   4. International trade.   I. Title.
      HC110.I5L346 2008
      339.2'20973—dc22   2007049601

Contents

Tables

Figures

Preface

Over the past quarter century, the US economy has generated a significant increase in output per worker, yet the typical worker has seen only a modest increase in take-home pay while the richest Americans have done exceedingly well. Although the reasons for these developments remain hotly disputed, many link them to the expansion of US trade, particularly with developing countries such as India and China. Public opinion polls indicate that there is widespread anxiety about trade among American workers, and politicians are thus expressing increasing skepticism about globalization.

Since standard economic theory predicts that foreign competition could have an adverse impact on the wages of less-skilled American workers, it is quite plausible to point to trade. But is trade really to blame? In this study, Institute Senior Fellow Robert Z. Lawrence explores the links between slow US real wage growth, increased earnings inequality, and trade and concludes that the latter has actually played a relatively minor role.

Lawrence first deconstructs the reported gap between real blue-collar wages and labor productivity growth over the past quarter century and estimates how much of the gap is due to measurement issues and how much higher these wages might have been had the distribution of income been kept constant. He demonstrates that about 60 percent of that gap reflects measurement issues, in particular, the use of different price deflators for output and real wages and the omission of benefits in take-home pay. He also finds that an additional 10 percent can be ascribed to the relatively rapid acquisition of skills by white-collar workers. However, he does conclude that three types of increased inequality account for about 30 percent of the gap: conventional wage inequality, which reflects an increase in the returns to skills; super rich inequality, which reflects the dramatic increase in wages of the richest Americans; and class inequality, which reflects the rising share of corporate profits in income. Lawrence considers what role trade is likely to have played for each type of inequality.

He suggests that increased trade with developing countries may indeed have played some part in causing greater wage inequality in the 1980s—although most studies point to technological change as a far more important reason. But its role more recently has been negligible. To be sure, since 1990, powerful globalization forces have been operating that might have been expected to increase wage inequality. Not only have imports from developing countries increased dramatically but the relative prices of manufactured goods from these countries have declined steadily. Yet the big surprise is that wages of the least-skilled Americans—the lowest 10 percent—have kept pace with the median and, since 1999, while real wage growth in general has been sluggish, most US relative wage and compensation measures indicate little evidence of increased inequality. This is true whether workers are distinguished by skill, education, unionization, occupation, or major sectors.

Apparently, the shocks from trade (or immigration) have not been large enough to increase conventional wage inequality. This is surprising given the growing scale of the competition from low-wage countries. Lawrence points out that some of the goods that the United States imports, even from developing countries, are quite sophisticated and are produced in the United States by relatively skilled workers. While other products may not be as sophisticated, the United States has adopted more skill-intensive and automated methods to produce them. Though it may cause displacement and could put downward pressure on wages generally, this import competition does not increase wage inequality.

A more benign view is that a significant amount of what America imports today is no longer produced domestically. Thus declining import prices simply yield consumer benefits but do not exert downward pressure on US wages nor cause dislocation of US workers. Paradoxically, therefore, globalization is actually causing less inequality because specialization is more advanced.

Lawrence also explores class inequality—changes in the income shares of profits and wages. Since 2000, labor's income share has fallen as wage increases have failed to match productivity growth almost across the entire spectrum of education levels. But it is hard to assign much of a role to trade since much of this drop appears to be cyclical—the low labor income share in 2006 was similar to that in 1997 and, over the long run, labor's share in US income has actually been quite stable.

The traditional channels that operate through trade also do not appear to be a disproportionately important driver of the growing share of income earned by the super rich. To be sure, "globalization" has played some role in increasing the size of relevant markets and thus incomes of CEOs, sports stars, entertainers, and software producers. But remarkably, the share of total US profits earned abroad by US multinationals has remained fairly constant. Far more important sources of this inequality are technological changes, institutional developments such as financial deregulation, modifications in US corporate governance practices, and rising asset markets, most of which have domestic origins.

Finally, it should be emphasized that the study does not dispute the importance of growing US inequality and the need for policies to deal with it, which the Institute had developed through numerous earlier publications and continues to actively support. But Lawrence provides compelling evidence that those seeking to give trade a prominent role in the explanation are looking in the wrong place.

The Peter G. Peterson Institute for International Economics is a private, nonprofit institution for the study and discussion of international economic policy. Its purpose is to analyze important issues in that area and to develop and communicate practical new approaches for dealing with them. The Institute is completely nonpartisan.

The Institute is funded by a highly diversified group of philanthropic foundations, private corporations, and interested individuals. About 30 percent of the Institute's resources in our latest fiscal year were provided by contributors outside the United States, including about 12 percent from Japan.

The Institute's Board of Directors bears overall responsibilities for the Institute and gives general guidance and approval to its research program, including the identification of topics that are likely to become important over the medium run (one to three years) and that should be addressed by the Institute. The director, working closely with the staff and outside Advisory Committee, is responsible for the development of particular projects and makes the final decision to publish an individual study.

The Institute hopes that its studies and other activities will contribute to building a stronger foundation for international economic policy around the world. We invite readers of these publications to let us know how they think we can best accomplish this objective.

C. FRED BERGSTEN
Director
December 2007

Acknowledgments

I am grateful for research assistance to Magali Junowicz and Sandro Parodi, for copyediting to Madona Devasahayam, and for comments from C. Fred Bergsten and participants in seminars at the Kennedy School of Government, Brandeis University, and the Peterson Institute for International Economics.

1

Introduction

Judging by the aggregate job numbers, American workers should have been pleased with the US economy's performance in 2006, but they were not. Their concerns were not related to jobs but to wages. The economy had fully recovered from the 2001 recession and was generating substantial employment growth—2 million additional jobs between 2005 and 2006—and the unemployment rate at 4.5 percent was close to what many considered to be the lowest level compatible with stable inflation. But for several years, wage and salary growth for all but the highest earners had been poor.

An astonishingly small fraction of workers—just the 3.4 percent with doctorates and professional graduate degrees (JDs, MBAs, and MDs)—fell in a category that sustained an increase in average inflation-adjusted take-home pay between 2000 and 2006. For workers with a college education, the slow real wage growth was a new experience because these workers had seen their real pay rise steadily between 1980 and 2000. But for most other workers, the recent weak wage growth continued a long-run trend in which, with the exception of the late 1990s, average hourly wages had failed to grow.

At the same time as wages were stagnating, though, rich Americans were clearly getting richer. In 2006 the share of corporate profits in national income was close to the highest levels since 1947 (figure 1.1). This inequality was reflected not just in the behavior of profits: The share of wage income reported in the top 1 percent of US tax returns in 2005 was almost double that recorded in 1980 (figure 1.2).

Contrasting the growth in output per hour with real average hourly earnings over the past quarter century vividly illustrates the concern about the fate of the typical American worker (figure 1.3). One might have

Figure 1.1   Share of corporate profits in US national income, 1947–2006

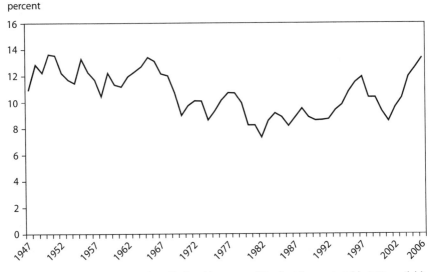

percent

Source: Bureau of Economic Analysis, National Income and Product Accounts, table 1.12, available at www.bea.gov.

expected the two series to track each other.[1] Yet, they tell strikingly different stories. Labor productivity growth was robust, and output per hour rose by over 50 logarithmic points, or 70 percent.[2] By contrast, average real hourly wages were virtually flat: Measured in 1982 dollars, the series increased just 4.4 percent—averaging $7.88 in 1981 and $8.23 in 2006.[3] Contrasting productivity growth with real annual male earnings tells a similar story: Measured in 2005 dollars, the median annual earnings of full-time male workers of $41,386 were actually below the $41,763 earned in 1980 (US Census Bureau 2005, table A-2, 38). Figure 1.3 also shows real

---

1. In principle, under competitive conditions, workers will be paid their marginal not average product, implying that output per worker need not always rise at the same rate as the marginal product of labor. However, as noted by Robert Topol in his lucid exposition of this issue in his comments on Dew-Becker and Gordon (2005, 135), "The observation that labor's share is fairly constant is one of the foundations of modern theories of economic growth." In general, factor shares in income will remain constant either if the elasticity of substitution is unity—i.e., the production function is Cobb-Douglas or if the supply of capital is perfectly elastic.

2. I use log point measures for expositional purposes. Small changes are close to percent changes.

3. In fact, in 1982 dollars, real hourly wages in 1964 were $7.82, and real weekly earnings in 1964 of $302 were actually higher than earnings in 1987 (Council of Economic Advisers, *Economic Report of the President 2006*, 338).

Figure 1.2 Share of top 1 percent workers in tax return wage income, 1980–2006

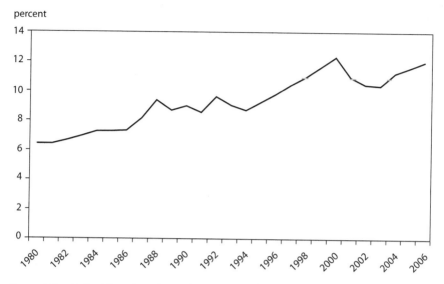

percent

Source: Data obtained from the website of Emmanuel Saez and Thomas Piketty, http://elsa.berkeley.edu/~saez.

wages of blue-collar workers,[4] taken from the employment cost index of the Bureau of Labor Statistics—a series that behaves similarly to average hourly earnings and is used extensively later in this policy analysis.

At face value, the picture suggests something was seriously amiss. On average, workers were producing considerably more, yet most workers seemed to have little to show for it. Where was the rest of the income generated by increased productivity going?[5] The plausible explanation is associated with rising inequality as others receive bigger pieces of the income pie: In particular, despite its name, the *average* hourly wage series actually provides an incomplete picture of worker wages because it reflects only the pay of *nonsupervisory* workers, who are paid by the hour and excludes workers in sales, managerial, professional, and technical occupations.

One possible answer is that the difference between nonsupervisory worker wages and total output was going into the (rapidly increasing)

---

4. Blue-collar workers comprise four major occupational categories: precision production craft and repair; machine operators, assemblers, and inspectors; transportation and material moving and handlers; and equipment cleaners, helpers, and laborers. In 1990 they constituted 29.8 percent of the labor force. See Schwink (1997).

5. Indeed, according to Robert Gordon and Ian Dew-Becker (2005), "half of the income gains went to the top 10 percent of the income distribution, leaving little left over for the bottom 90 percent."

Figure 1.3 Business-sector output per hour and real hourly wages, 1981–2006

log points (1981 = 0)

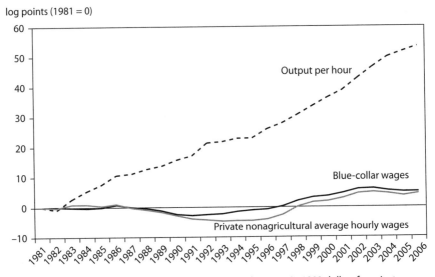

Note: Output per hour for business sector; average hourly wages in 1982 dollars for private non-agricultural industries; employment cost index for blue-collar wages in 1982 dollars.

Source: Bureau of Labor Statistics.

compensation of the workers whose earnings are excluded when average hourly wages are calculated. A second possibility is that the difference was going into the wage compensation of the very rich 1 percent of workers such as chief executive officers (CEOs) and others who command especially high salaries and whose pay often includes stock options. Most labor earnings measures also do not accurately reflect these earnings. A third possibility is that the difference was going into profits or other forms of capital income. Chapter 2 provides quantitative estimates of the role each of these three components has played in increasing income inequality.

What explains this weak wage growth? One answer often given is globalization. At the same time as inequality has increased, the United States has certainly become more integrated into the global economy. This correlation leads many to ascribe causation. The sum of exports and imports of goods and services has increased from 20 percent of GDP in 1980 to 28 percent of GDP in 2005 (figure 1.4), with recent import growth heavily concentrated in goods and services from developing countries. International financial markets have also undergone explosive growth. US multinationals have continued to expand abroad, and many domestic firms have increased their reliance on offshored inputs. The United States has also become the world's largest recipient of inward foreign direct invest-

Figure 1.4 Goods and services trade as a share of US GDP, 1978–2006

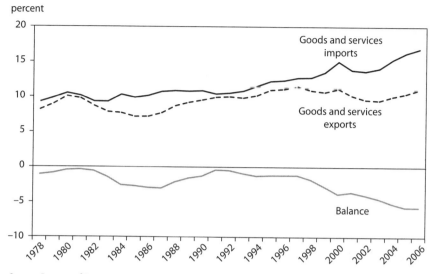

percent

Source: Bureau of Economic Analysis, National Income and Product Accounts, tables 1.1.5 and 4.1, available at www.bea.gov.

ment.[6] Moreover, improvements in computing and telecommunications now make it possible to transmit a wide range of services across the globe instantaneously and at low cost.

It is fairly widely accepted that in the aggregate, trade generates gains and promotes economic growth,[7] but trade can also create winners and losers. In America's case, trade with developing countries could be particularly problematic because it could put downward pressures on the earnings of lower-wage workers. And indeed, it is precisely this type of trade that has expanded especially rapidly over the past decade, partly because countries such as China and India have emerged as major global competitors and partly because the United States has vigorously imple-

---

6. Employment in foreign affiliates of US multinationals was up 51 percent between 1982 and 2004 (Bureau of Economic Analysis, *Survey of Current Business*, November 2006). Employment in nonbank majority-owned US affiliates of foreign companies increased by 68 percent between 1988 and 2003 (Bureau of Economic Analysis, *Survey of Current Business,* August 2005).

7. Exporting raises the prices producers can charge for their products and allows for economies of scale. Importing reduces product prices and increases the choices available to consumers. Trade may also intensify competition, thereby encouraging firms to be more productive and innovative. According to one recent estimate, US incomes are about 10 percent higher than they would be if the economy were self-sufficient. See Bradford, Grieco, and Hufbauer (2005).

mented free trade agreements with Mexico (the North American Free Trade Agreement) and other developing countries.

The views of Stephen Roach, chief economist at Morgan Stanley, are typical:

> Globalization hasn't exactly lived up to its win-win billing. While the developing world has benefited from the first win, in the rich countries the spoils of the second win have gone mainly to the owners of capital. . . . The global labor arbitrage has put unrelenting pressure on employment and real wages in the high-cost developed world. (Roach 2006)

Similarly, in a recent column, Paul Krugman emphasized the role of China and the increased possibility of trading services and concluded:

> It's no longer safe to assert that trade's impact on the income distribution in wealthy countries is fairly minor. There's a good case that it is big, and getting bigger. . . . It's clear that applying the same models to current data that, for example, led William Cline of the Peterson Institute to conclude in 1997 that trade was responsible for a 6% widening in the college-high school gap would lead to a much larger estimate today. (Krugman 2007)

To be sure, many acknowledge that factors other than globalization (e.g., technological changes, deunionization, changing social norms,[8] modifications in US corporate governance, deindustrialization, and immigration) are causing inequality to rise. Nonetheless, there is polling evidence that Americans are becoming increasingly disenchanted with trade. A 2000 Gallup poll found that 56 percent of respondents saw trade as an opportunity and 36 percent saw it as a threat—but by 2005, the respective percentages shifted to 44 and 49 percent, respectively (Slaughter and Scheve 2007). Especially noteworthy is the drop in support from Americans with college education, a development that has been associated with their sluggish real wage growth.

Some say that precisely because these other forces are at work, the additional pressures due to trade liberalization with developing countries are particularly inopportune and are calling for a "time out" with respect to new trade agreements. Several Democratic candidates for president are opposed to the bilateral trade agreements the George W. Bush administration has negotiated with Peru, Panama, Colombia, and South Korea. And President Bush has had difficulty in renewing his trade promotion authority. Given the fact that the developing countries in particular are awaiting a successful conclusion of the Doha Round, which is supposed to emphasize their needs, these views could be consequential.

This policy analysis explores the links between international trade and increased income inequality. It deconstructs the gap between real blue-

---

8. For an illuminating analysis of the role of norms and institutions, see Levy and Temin (2007).

collar wages and labor productivity growth and estimates how much higher these wages might have been had income growth been distributed proportionately and how much of the gap is due to measurement and technical factors about which little can be done. It argues that while increased trade with developing countries may have played some part in causing greater inequality in the 1980s, surprisingly, over the past decade the impact of such trade on inequality has been relatively small.

Distinctions and Qualifications

Before proceeding with the analysis, several prefatory distinctions should be made. First, as this discussion has already implied, the nature of US inequality is complex. While they may be related at times, at least three kinds of inequality need to be distinguished: wage inequality (i.e., increased pay differentials for workers with different levels of education, skill, experience, and other characteristics), super rich inequality (i.e., increase in the income share of the very top wage earners, whose incomes are often heavily related to stock market performance through stock options), and class inequality (i.e., increase in the share of income earned by owners of capital—in particular, corporate profits).

Over the past 25 years, all three types of inequality have increased in the United States, but they have emerged at different times. Moreover, wage inequality in particular has taken different forms. There was a pervasive increase in wage inequality in the 1980s associated with skill levels. In the 1990s, however, wages near the top of the income distribution (90th percentile) continued to rise more rapidly than wages at the median, but wages at the bottom of the distribution kept up or actually increased faster than wages in the middle. Since 2000, with the exception of the very top, wages have generally moved in tandem, meaning that over the past 25 years, blue-collar workers—particularly those with a high school education or less—have fared poorly while college-educated workers have done relatively well. But over the past six years, almost all workers, including those with college degrees, have done poorly.

Increased super rich inequality also occurred in spurts between 1985 and 1988 and again in the late 1990s, while class inequality appeared only after 2000. Many discussions confound these forms of inequality, but as the timing suggests, they are likely to stem from different causes and in particular to be affected differently by international factors in general and trade and trade agreements in particular.

Another key distinction is between inequality and poverty. While the poorest working Americans did do relatively badly in the 1980s, wage data suggest that since the early 1990s, they have actually been doing comparatively well. This improvement shows up in wages in the 50th percentile rising more slowly than those in the 10th percentile and in the wages of high school dropouts rising as rapidly as the wages of high school graduates. It also shows up in the relatively strong rise in real incomes of households with children in the lowest quintile.[9] While the rich are getting (relatively) richer, the poor are not getting (relatively) poorer! Thus the inequality that has arisen is between the very rich and the middle class. This development has important implications for concerns about immigration and low-wage competition.

As mentioned earlier, the discussion on the causes of inequality often refers very loosely to globalization, which is sometimes used as a synonym for structural change. But such references can be a very misleading and dangerous oversimplification, particularly if it leads to policy prescriptions that are motivated by the belief that protectionism could effectively reverse the rise in inequality. The US economy is linked to the rest of the world through trade in goods and services and flows of capital—both direct and indirect foreign investment—and through the international diffusion of technology and other forms of communication. And any or all of these connections could influence the US distribution of income.

In this study, however, I focus mainly on one of these links, international trade, since the current policy debate seems to focus primarily on trade agreements and expansion. But even with respect to trade, chains of causation are complex. Trade is not really an independent variable that one can talk accurately of as necessarily "causing anything" nor can one readily separate trade from other sources of structural change.[10] Faster growth in China or changes in its domestic policies could lead it to trade more with the United States. A crop failure in the United States could lead to more trade. A new trade agreement could lead to more trade, and technological discoveries in the United States could be encouraged by the country's ability to trade and thus result in more trade. All these can affect trade but have quite different effects on the distribution of income.

Inequality, in turn, can be measured in a number of ways. One key distinction is between income and wealth. Given rapid increases in asset prices, such as equity and real estate, the distribution of wealth in the United States has become even more unequal than the distribution of income. But to keep the scope of the study manageable, I consider only income. In addition, I concentrate on individual pretax incomes. Income inequality is sometimes measured at the level of the family and sometimes the household, and the levels at which this measurement is done

---

9. A recent Congressional Budget Office (CBO 2007) study, for example, finds that households with children in the lowest quintile have had real income increases of 35 percent between 1991 and 2006, faster than all but the highest quintile.

10. For an excellent discussion of the endogenous nature of trade, see Deardorff and Hakura (1994).

can make a huge difference.[11] Decisions on how much to work and whom to marry or live with can alter the link between individual earnings and household incomes.[12]

Similarly, incomes can be affected not only by earnings but also by taxes and transfers. But I focus on pretax and transfer individual earnings because these are most likely to be directly affected by pressures operating through international trade. Earnings are also affected both by how much people work and by what they earn by hour. Trade could affect both, but its major impact is likely to be on factor prices, and thus wherever possible, in considering labor income the study uses data on hourly earnings.

I should also emphasize that, although the terms "equity" and "equality" are sometimes used interchangeably, by focusing on inequality, however, I do not mean to imply it is always undesirable. Higher incomes could, of course, be derived through exploiting others and through unfair behavior, but they could also be an appropriate reward for obtaining new skills and/or working harder and smarter in activities that also increase the welfare of others. Nonetheless, keeping in mind the importance of providing incentives for greater productivity, it might still be appropriate to ask those who make more to pay proportionately more in taxes.

For much of the study I adopt the perspective of a typical blue-collar US worker. The central question I ask is, how much better off would this worker have been had income inequality not increased? Answering this question requires not only comparing the relative growth of this worker's earnings to those of richer workers but also taking account of how much additional income would have been available to individual blue-collar workers had inequality not increased. In other words, what is important is not simply the percentage increase in the relative earnings of one group compared with another, but what share of total income this increase constitutes.

Finally, I argue that trade with developing countries is not a particularly important contributor to US inequality. But I do not intend to imply either that trade has played no role at all in these developments or that, more

---

11. This distinction may be important. According to Peter Gottschalk and Sheldon Danziger (2003), the 1990s were a period in which wages became more equal but family income inequality continued to increase. For the purposes of this policy analysis, the focus will be on wages and incomes.

12. Gottschalk and Danziger (2003) write: ". . . long-run changes in society's living arrangements have taken place, also tending to exacerbate household income differences. For example, divorces, marital separations, births out of wedlock, and increasing age at first marriage have led to a shift away from married-couple households to single-parent families and nonfamily households. Since non-married-couple households tend to have lower income and income that is less equally distributed than other types of households (partly because of the likelihood of fewer earners in them), changes in household composition have been associated with growing income inequality."

Table 1.1   Accounting for the gap between real wage and labor productivity growth, 1981–2006

Source	Log points
Growth in real ECI blue-collar wages, 1981–2006	4.9
Growth in business-sector output per hour, 1981–2006	53.3
Difference	48.4
Due to	
Technical factors	33.8
Of which	
Benefits (compensation versus take-home pay)	11.9
Prices (product versus consumption)	17.7
Skills (relatively rapid white-collar skills growth)	4.2
Inequality	14.6
Of which	
Wage inequality	6.8
Super rich inequality	3.1
Class inequality (profits)	4.7

ECI = employment cost index

generally, increasing US income inequality or the dislocation of US workers, firms, and communities are not serious issues that require policy responses. To the contrary, I hope that by understanding that trade is not the major driver, either of inequality or displacement, US policymakers will be led to focus on crafting effective policy responses to these problems rather than taking counterproductive or ineffective protectionist actions.

Plan of the Study

Chapter 2 quantifies the sources of the gap between blue-collar wages and productivity over the past 25 years. These sources are decomposed into those that actually do result from greater inequality and those that reflect measurement issues (table 1.1 and appendix table A.1). Two measurement issues account for 60 percent of the 48.4-log-point gap—i.e., 29.6 log points. The first is that the wage measures fail to take account of benefits; the second is that the real wage and output per worker measures are obtained using different price deflators. Another 10 percent of the gap—4.2 log points—reflects the increased skills of non-blue-collar workers. About half of the remaining 14.6 log points (6.8 log points) is attributable to higher wage inequality—i.e., relatively more rapid increases in non-blue-collar hourly wages—with the remainder split between increased wage earnings of the super rich (3.1 log points) and recent increases in profits (4.7 log points).

Chapter 3 deals with both the theory and evidence on the links between trade and wage inequality. Conventional trade theory predicts that wage inequality along the lines of skill could increase in developed countries if either they or developing countries liberalize. Most of the studies that test the theory conclude that trade has indeed played some role in the United States—typically on the order of about 10 to 20 percent of the historic increase in the ratio of the wages of skilled to unskilled worker. Though some studies argue for larger effects, almost all find that in raising skill premiums, skill-biased technological change was far more important than trade.

But almost all studies focused on the period through the mid-1990s, and the experience between 1999 and 2006 has been different: By many quantity and price indicators, powerful globalization forces were operating during this period. Yet US relative wage and compensation measures indicate very little evidence of increased inequality by skill, education, unionization, or occupation and sector—indeed, if anything, compensation in manufacturing increased relatively rapidly. Apparently, neither trade nor technological change (nor anything else) has continued to increase conventional wage inequality.[13]

This is surprising given the growing scale of competition from low-wage countries. There are three lines of explanation: One is that the goods that the United States imports are actually very sophisticated and produced in the United States by relatively skilled workers. While it may cause displacement and could put downward pressure on wages generally, competition from low-wage countries does not increase wage inequality. A second more benign view is that a significant amount of what America imports today is no longer produced domestically. Thus, declining import prices simply yield consumer benefits and do not exert downward pressure on US wages or cause dislocation of US workers. A third view is that while US imports may be produced using labor-intensive methods abroad, when produced in the United States, capital- and skilled-labor-intensive methods are used.

It appears that US trade today combines these elements in proportions that are hard to disentangle, particularly at levels of disaggregation that allow for a sufficiently precise matching of products and the wages earned in producing them. At relatively high levels of aggregation, the data indicate that manufactured imports overall, and even those from developing countries such as China and Mexico, are concentrated in US manufacturing sectors that pay significantly higher than average US wages. This means that import displacement does not fall disproportionately on less-skilled workers. While there has been considerable displacement from trade during this period, it has not increased wage inequality.

---

13. There is still some evidence of wages rising relatively rapidly recently for those with advanced degrees (or at or above the 90th percentile).

At more disaggregated levels, however, the data reveal that goods imported from developing countries such as China *are* associated with relatively less-skilled labor inputs and—judging by their unit values—are qualitatively different from those produced by developed countries such as the United States. This provides support for the view that much of this trade reflects more complete specialization and as such does not result in either wage inequality or downward pressure on wages generally.

Chapter 4 explores class inequality—changes in the income shares of profits and wages. Since 2000, labor's income share has fallen as wage increases have failed to match productivity growth almost across the entire spectrum of education levels. This decline could, in principle, be the result of increased trade pressures such as offshoring, which raises profits and reduces wages in part through affecting labor's bargaining power.

But there are reasons to be skeptical. First, the low labor income share in 2006 was actually similar to that in 1997, suggesting a strong cyclical component in recent performance. Second, while it is plausible that labor's bargaining power and labor rents could be reduced by the ability to offshore, there was no such decline in labor share over either the 1980s or 1990s. Third, if offshoring to China and other developing countries were the major driver of labor's depressed share, the fall would be especially apparent in tradable goods, but recent profit growth has not been especially concentrated in manufacturing. Indeed, it has been concentrated in financial corporations. In fact, between 2000 and 2005, the share of compensation in manufacturing (or traded goods) did not decline more rapidly than in the rest of private industry, and manufacturing compensation has actually increased relatively more rapidly than compensation in general.

Similarly, offshoring of services, for example, to India, has actually been much smaller than public headlines suggest and too small to account for the pervasive slow real wage growth since 2000. A crucial question that will be resolved only as the current expansion matures is, how much of the recent shift is simply cyclical and how much could reflect a new version of Stolper-Samuelson effects in which trade liberalization operates by raising the relative price of capital-intensive goods.

Chapter 5 considers super rich inequality. The traditional channels that operate through trade do not appear to be an important driver of this development. Globalization more broadly construed has played some role in increasing the size of relevant markets and thus incomes of CEOs, sports stars, entertainers, and software producers. But this effect does not seem to be disproportionately large. Remarkably, the share of income and value-added produced by US multinational corporations in their overseas affiliates has remained fairly constant as has the share of US corporate profits earned abroad. Super rich inequality is also being driven by technological changes, institutional developments such as financial deregulation, changes in US corporate governance practices, and rising asset markets, most of which have domestic origins.

Chapter 6 briefly considers a second source of worker anxiety: job loss and dislocation. Trade is found to have been a factor in the dislocation of manufacturing workers, but it is only one of a host of forces causing job loss. Some dislocation in the future could also occur as a result of increased electronic offshoring. While such offshoring could be extremely painful for the workers involved, in aggregate terms the US labor force should be able to adjust to these changes without disruption that is unusually large in historic terms.

The central conclusion of the study is that international trade is responsible for a relatively small share of growing income inequality and labor-market displacement in the United States. Even if this study had concluded that trade was a major cause, it would not necessarily have followed that increased trade protection would be the correct policy response. But the minor role played by trade suggests that any policy that focuses narrowly on trade to deal with these problems is likely to be ineffective. Instead, the response should be (a) to use the tax system to improve income distribution and (b) to implement adjustment policies to deal more generally with worker and community dislocation.

2

The Wage-Productivity Gap, 1981–2006

This chapter focuses on the earnings of US workers in blue-collar occupations.[1] I show that while about 30 percent of the gap between wages and productivity between 1981 and 2006 is associated with increased inequality, much of it reflects measurement issues.

The blue-collar group includes craft workers, operatives, and laborers, most of whom have less than a college degree and whose earnings are relatively concentrated in the middle of the earnings distribution.[2] The employment cost index (ECI) from the Bureau of Labor Statistics (BLS) for these workers is ideal for exploring these earnings because it is a fixed weight series that captures pure wage changes and is in principle unaffected by shifts in labor force composition among workers between occupations and industries.[3]

In fact, as shown in figure 1.3, over the 1981–2006 period, the blue-collar ECI wage series actually behaved very similar to the average hourly wage series for all nonsupervisory workers. The ECI indicates that real

---

1. For a similar analysis, see Rose (2007).

2. In 2006, for example, less than 7 percent of workers in blue-collar occupations had a college degree compared with 30 percent in the overall labor force (Bureau of Labor Statistics and US Census Bureau, Current Population Survey, Educational Attainment data, available at www.census.gov). Estimates based on Llg (2006) indicate that in 2000, 60 percent of these workers' earnings fell between the 25th and 75th percentiles of national earnings.

3. The ECI measures quarterly changes in compensation costs for civilian workers (nonfarm private industry and state and local government workers). The ECI uses data collected from business establishments, which are weighted to represent the universe of establishments and occupations at a particular point in time.

wages of blue-collar occupations increased by just 4.9 log points between 1981 and 2006. (Over the same period, real average hourly wages were up 4.34 log points.) By contrast, output per hour in the business sector was up 53.3 log points—a 48.4-log-point gap (figure 1.3).

My analysis of this gap involves five steps. First, it is necessary to deal with two measurement issues: One is that real wages and real outputs are deflated with different price measures and another is that wages do not include benefits. Second, the role played by wage inequality (i.e., blue-collar versus other wages) can be estimated by comparing the growth in blue-collar wages with that of the overall ECI. Third, the effects of changing labor force skill composition must be taken into account. Fourth, the role of profits can be obtained by comparing the growth of business-sector value-added with the most comprehensive measure of business-sector compensation. Finally, the share of labor income going to wages that are not included in the ECI can be obtained as a residual.

Measurement Adjustments

When one contrasts measures of real wages and output per worker and implies that they should rise in tandem, one is basically comparing apples and oranges. Even aside from the fact that in theory these could deviate for reasons such as differences between the average and marginal product of labor, two important measurement issues should not be overlooked.

Benefits

The cost of employing a worker that firms will, in principle, equate to the worker's marginal product is not only the take-home pay but also the other benefits the worker receives in the form of Social Security contributions, life insurance, retirement benefits, and health care. Over much of the 1981–2006 period, benefits have been rising faster than wages, which implies that the wage growth alone underestimates the full value of increases in worker pay. The practice of referring to hourly wages (or take-home incomes) without accounting for these benefits is a serious omission, not only for measures of take-home pay such as average hourly earnings but also for many of the household income measures that are frequently taken as indicating trends both in real incomes and inequality.

The same is true of the many studies of wage trends undertaken by labor economists and others using the BLS and Census Bureau's Current Population Survey (CPS) data. If benefits such as health care are relatively similar for high- and low- or (more likely) median-wage workers and if they are shifted backward into wages, their rapid growth could well in-

Figure 2.1   Blue-collar pay and business-sector output per hour, 1981–2006

log points (1981 = 0)

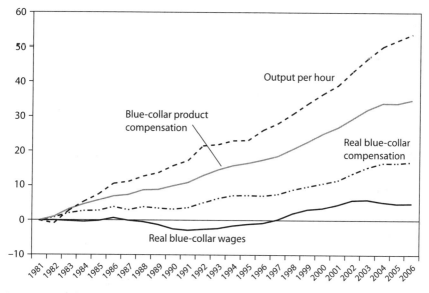

Source: Bureau of Labor Statistics, Employment Cost Index, Consumer Price Index, and Productivity and Related Data on the Business Sector, available at www.bls.gov.

crease wage inequality, even though compensation inequality was unaffected.[4] Moreover, if workers at the bottom are more likely to have lost their benefits over time, then considering only their wage increases could overstate the increase in their compensation.

However, the full costs of nonwage benefits *are* taken account of in measures of total compensation. By using the real ECI for blue-collar compensation, which includes benefits, and comparing it with the corresponding real ECI for blue-collar wages, one can readily estimate the difference taking account of benefits makes. As indicated in figure 2.1, between 1981 and 2006, the rise in the real ECI for blue-collar compensation was 16.8 log points—compared with just a 4.9-log-point increase for real blue-collar wages. This implies that increased benefits account for 11.9 log points—roughly a quarter—of the 48.4-log-point gap. Taking account of benefits also indicates there has been less "wage" inequality than the take-home pay (wage) data indicate. Between 1981 and 2006, for example,

---

4. For the theory of shifting of benefits, see Summers (1989). For evidence on the incidence of health benefits, see Baicker and Chandra (2006).

while blue-collar wages fell by 14 log points relative to white-collar wages, blue-collar compensation fell by only 11 log points relative to white-collar compensation.[5]

Deflators

A second measurement issue relates to the way in which output per worker and compensation are deflated to get real measures. Economic theory predicts that under competitive conditions, the wage rate (w) should equal marginal value product, which is marginal product (MP) times the product price (P)—i.e., $w = MP \times P$. The relevant real wage ($w/P = MP$) that should track marginal product is known as the product wage—i.e., nominal wage rate divided by the prices of the products that workers actually produce. It is a production concept. By contrast, the "real wage" that is generally quoted is a consumption concept and measures what workers can buy. It is measured by deflating the wage rate by the consumer price index.

Both the weights and composition of the business-sector price deflator (PBUS) used to measure productivity and the consumer price index used to measure real wages are different. Over the past 25 years, the prices of goods and services workers actually produced in the business sector have risen more slowly than the prices of goods and services workers consume. In particular, the PBUS has a higher weight for investment goods (such as computers and machinery, whose prices have risen slowly—or even declined) while the consumer price index gives a larger weight to housing and imports (such as petroleum), whose prices have increased more rapidly.[6]

When measures of real output that deflate nominal output by the PBUS are compared with those of real wages that deflate nominal wages by the consumer price index), the productivity-wage gap is exaggerated. The difference between the growth in the two series between 1981 and 2006 amounts to 17.7 log points. Thus, taking account of the faster growth in the costs of benefits and using the PBUS to measure the real (product) compensation of blue-collar workers, I find an increase in the ECI for blue-collar compensation of 34.5 log points rather than just 4.9 log points (figure 2.1).

Thus, these two adjustments (11.9 log points for benefits and 17.7 log points for deflators) explain about 60 percent of the gap—i.e., 29.6 log

---

5. By contrast, Brooks Pierce (2001) reports a greater increase in compensation inequality than in wage inequality between 1981 and 1997, but as suggested by figure 4.3, which shows several cycles in the share of benefits in compensation, this finding is likely to be very sensitive to the observation period. Over the 1981–2006 period as a whole, there is a clear upward trend in the share of benefits in compensation.

6. For more detail, see Lawrence and Slaughter (1993) and Bosworth and Perry (1994).

points. This estimate means that in fact, blue-collar workers have actually made significant real gains over the past 20 years. Certainly, their earnings have lagged behind those of white-collar workers (up 46 log points over the same period when similarly deflated) and behind productivity growth, but they have averaged roughly 1.5 percent per year in real (product) terms and are not as inconsequential as might be inferred from the average hourly wage series. But it still leaves 18.8 log points unaccounted for.

Role of Wage Inequality

Using the ECI measures, I estimate the role of increased wage inequality in explaining the blue-collar wage-productivity gap. Between 1981 and 2006, deflated by the PBUS, the ECI for blue-collar compensation increased by 34.5 log points. When similarly deflated, the aggregate ECI increased by 41.3 log points. Since both these are fixed weight measures, these differences reflect pure compensation price effects. If there had been no change in relative compensation between 1981 and 2006 and all workers had received the average increase, blue-collar workers would have been 6.8 log points better off (41.3 log points minus 34.5 log points). This is my estimate of the impact of wage inequality.

Rise in Skills of Non-Blue-Collar Workers

Relative increases in worker skills is another element to be considered. Education is likely to make workers more productive. For example, if one out of 10 workers with only a high school education obtained a college education, the earnings of that worker would be expected to increase. One would also expect total and average output per worker to increase. But one would not expect the wages of the nine other workers to rise. Thus, if some workers are improving their skills particularly rapidly either because of education or experience, then it could be a reason why wages of *other* workers (i.e., those not experiencing such improvements) might not rise as fast as overall output per worker.

In fact, the United States has undergone precisely such a change over the 1981–2006 period. Between 1981 and 2005, for example, the share of blue-collar workers in the labor force fell from 31 to 24 percent, and high-wage (and thus high-skilled) occupations expanded relatively rapidly.[7] Moreover, the growth in the share of white-collar workers with a college education was much larger than the growth in the share of blue-collar workers with a college education. Thus, one would expect the relative

---

7. See US Census Bureau, *Statistical Abstract of the United States, 2007*, table 605 on Occupations of the Employed by Selected Characteristics, available at www.census.gov.

increase in the share of college-educated workers in the white-collar labor force to account for some part of the gap. But how much adjustment should be made for these changes in labor force composition?

The BLS takes account of changes in labor force composition when estimating multifactor productivity.[8] Instead of simply entering hours as a crude measure of labor input, the bureau derives a labor input measure that accounts for changes in labor force quality. In undertaking this estimate, the BLS classifies workers by a number of characteristics (experience, education, and sex for males and in addition, for females, number of children and marital status). It then weights the growth rates in the hours of different types of workers by their share in total compensation. It uses a Tornqvist chained index to estimate changes in the quality of labor inputs annually.[9] This implies that over time the BLS measure will capture *both* changes in the relative supplies of different types of workers and changes in their relative wages.[10] All told, over the 1981–2006 period, this measure increased by 12.4 log points.

Since I am interested in changes in the skill levels of non-blue-collar workers, this measure is not exactly what I want. First, because it captures *both* changes in relative wages of different types of workers and changes in skills and second, because it takes account of changes in the composition of the *entire* labor force and thus includes the impact of improvements in the composition of blue-collar workers as well as other workers. But I can use the BLS measure to get a rough estimate of what I am interested in by making two adjustments to remove these effects.

I require an estimate of the impact of pure price changes on relative wages. I have already obtained this estimate by comparing the behavior of the real product blue-collar compensation with the behavior of the overall real product ECI for all private industry.[11] This comparison yielded 6.8 log

---

8. These estimates are available at the Bureau of Labor Statistics website at www.bls.gov/mfp.

9. The hours at work for each of the 1,008 types of workers classified by their educational attainment, work experience, and gender are aggregated using an annually chained (Tornqvist) index. The growth rate of the aggregate is, therefore, a weighted average of the growth rates of each type of worker, where the weight assigned to a type of worker is its share of total labor compensation. The resulting aggregate measure of labor input accounts for both the increase in raw hours at work and changes in the skill composition (as measured by education and work experience) of the workforce.

10. "The weights can change from year to year because of shifts in the relative compensation of groups of workers. For example, the earnings of college graduates have increased faster than the earnings of high school graduates since the early 1970s. As a result, the share of compensation and the weight on the rapidly growing hours of college graduates has increased and spurred labor composition growth in the 1980s" (Bureau of Labor Statistics, *Labor Input and Labor Composition Growth*, chapter 2, 13).

11. Another possibility that was considered was to compare the ECI with the Employer Costs for Employee Compensation (ECEC), which uses a similar sample but reflects actual costs rather than fixed weights and therefore could indicate the effects of changes in composition. However, inconsistencies in methodologies make this comparison inappropriate.

points as an estimate of the impact of changes captured by relative wage changes over the period. This estimate suggests that 5.6 log points (12.4 minus 6.8) could be ascribed to additional improvements in total labor force composition. However, this number also includes the improvements in the composition (educational level, etc.) of the blue-collar labor force. Accordingly, I mark down this measure by 27.5 percent throughout the period to reflect the improvements in the composition of the blue-collar workforce.[12] This markdown suggests that over the entire period, 4.2 log points (0.75 × 5.6) can be ascribed to non-blue-collar improvements in labor force composition.

Adding the 4.2-log-point estimate for the pure skills composition effect and the 6.8 log points for the effects of changes in relative wages to the previously obtained estimate of 34.5 for the increase in blue-collar compensation deflated by PBUS implies I can now account for 45.5 log points. However, I still need measures of the shares going to the very top wage earners and to profits to reach the 53.3 total for the increase in output per hour.

Profits and Top Wage Earners

The BLS Office of Productivity and Technology provides a second compensation measure known as hourly compensation.[13] This measure covers the business sector, but it differs from the ECI in not being a fixed weight index and in its coverage and type of compensation that it includes. In particular, it is more comprehensive because hourly compensation includes estimates of the value of labor services provided by business owners and others who set their own wages (e.g., CEOs)—a group that typically includes some very high-wage earners and is excluded from the ECI measure. In addition, hourly compensation takes account of compensation such as tips, and, importantly, stock options, which are not included in the ECI measure. In particular, the hourly compensation measure includes gains on so-called nonqualified stock options, which are counted as compensation when they are exercised, not when they are paid (Ruser 2001). This more comprehensive compensation series, when deflated by the PBUS, increases by 48.6 log points between 1981 and 2006. It is particularly useful for completing the gap puzzle.

On the one hand, since value-added is divided between profits and labor compensation, the difference between output per hour and this

---

12. The share of blue-collar workers has declined from 31 percent in 1981 to 24 percent in 2005 (Bureau of Labor Statistics and Census Bureau, Current Population Survey).

13. These measures of productivity and costs are available at the Bureau of Labor Statistics website, www.bls.gov/lpc.

series indicates the share of the gap attributable to profits. It implies that increased profit share can account for 4.7 log points (53.3 minus 48.6) of the gap. On the other hand, the difference between this comprehensive series (48.6) and the 45.5 log points I have already estimated—i.e., 3.1 log points—can be used as indicating the increase in private-sector compensation that is neither captured in the ECI nor attributable to increased skills. This difference likely includes the increased earnings of the richest American wage earners, many of whom are business proprietors and whose earnings may be particularly concentrated in stock options. Indeed, the correspondence between the robust growth in these earnings and the stock market boom in the late 1990s is particularly noteworthy. I will therefore refer to this difference as reflecting the increased earnings of the super rich, although some poorer workers earn tips and others have earned wage income in the form of exercised stock options, so this residual is likely to overstate their share.

Is my estimate of the share going to the super rich reasonable? The CPS of wages is top coded, and the earnings of workers above the highest threshold are simply entered as greater than a particular amount—say, $100,000. Accurate and comprehensive data for the super rich—those earning in the top 1 percent or so—can be obtained only from tax or Social Security returns.

However, even when referring only to wage incomes, these data will not be strictly comparable to the corporate-sector labor earnings data. First, the Internal Revenue Service (IRS) data are for tax returns rather than for individuals and include married couples and could therefore be affected by decisions on filing status. The Social Security data still include earnings of nonincorporated (self-employed) professionals. Another problem with both these data sources is that they may well be influenced by changes in the tax code, which could affect the decision to incorporate.

However, the estimate obtained above actually tracks those obtained using tax returns fairly well since 1990 but not before. According to that data assembled by Emmanuel Saez and Thomas Piketty, between 1990 and 2000, the share of the top 1 percent of tax filers in wage income increased from 8.99 to 12.33 percent, an increase of 3.34 percentage points.[14] According to my estimates, over the same period, the increase was 3.1 log points.

For the 1980s, however, my method fails to find a significant increase in super rich incomes, whereas they find an additional increase of 6.43 to 8.99 percent—i.e., 2.47 percent. Much of this change occurs between 1985 and 1988 and, as Alan Reynolds (2007) has pointed out, may heavily reflect a response to changes in the tax code, which reduced the top marginal tax bracket to 28 percent and thereby provided these taxpayers with

---

14. These income tax statistics are available at http://elsa.berkeley.edu/~saez.

Figure 2.2   Contributions of inequality to the productivity-wage gap, 1981–2006

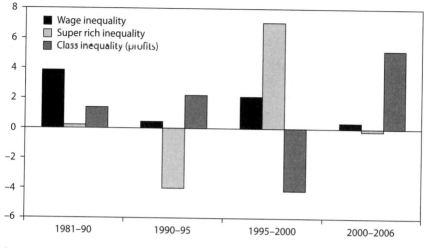

log points

Source: Appendix table A.1.

an incentive to shift their incomes from corporate to individual tax returns. But it should have been captured in the average hourly measure.[15]

Table 1.1 summarizes these estimates, and appendix table A.1 reports annual time-series in greater detail. For the full quarter century from 1981 to 2006, of the 48.4-log-point gap between productivity and real blue-collar wages, 33.8 points are not related to inequality. These reflect measurement issues (prices and benefits) and increased skills. The remaining 14.6 log points are associated with the three distinct forms of wage inequality: 6.8 log points is attributable to increased wage inequality as captured by the ECI, 3.1 log points to the residual—much of which accrues to the super rich—and 4.7 log points to the increase in profit share.

The timing of each form of inequality can be tracked as indicated in figure 2.2, which is derived from the data in appendix table A.1. And it is interesting that they do not correspond. The biggest changes in the impact of wage inequality took place in the 1980s (3.8 log points), although there were substantial increases in the second half of the 1990s as well (2.1 log points). By contrast, there has been almost no increase in the wage

---

15. The tax returns data show a large increase in the share of the top 1 percent in wages but also a major decline in the income share from capital. In 1982, for example, the top 1 percent received 48 percent of their income from capital income and dividends; by 1992, this income declined to 22 percent—similar to their current share. So clearly, there was massive reclassification, calling the long-run estimates into serious question.

inequality gap since 2000 (just 0.4 log points)—a remarkable result that I explore in some depth. The story for profits is the opposite: More than the full impact occurred between 2000 and 2005 (5.2 log points). The small increase in the 1980s and early 1990s was more than offset by a decline in the second half of the 1990s.

The super rich increases took place late in the second half of the 1990s, particularly when the stock market boomed. They then subsided during the recession and recovered between 2003 and 2006. Thus, if globalization or any other single cause is the source of all the inequality, it would have to be operating in very different ways over time, essentially affecting wage inequality mainly before 2000, super rich inequality mainly over the past decade, and profits/wages inequality after 2000.

Conclusion

In sum, this chapter has been an exercise in measurement. I have shown how the various aggregate data series compiled by the BLS can be used to derive a fairly complete accounting of the role of measurement factors, increased skills, and the three types of increased inequality in accounting for the gap between real blue-collar wages and output per hour over the past quarter century. The approach is useful in providing some perspective both on the relative magnitudes and on the timing of these different forces at play.

Overall, it suggests that about 70 percent of the gap has nothing to do with inequality, but the remaining 30 percent (14.6 log points) can be ascribed to wage inequality (6.8 log points), class or profits inequality (4.7 log points), and the super rich (3.1 log points). In the rest of this analysis, I ask what role international trade is likely to have played in generating each type of inequality.

3

Wage Inequality and Trade

Wage inequality emerged in the United States when it had become more open to trade and many developing countries were liberalizing their trade regimes. It is not surprising, therefore, that many observers argued that these developments were causally connected. Indeed, conventional trade theory would predict exactly such a connection.

I will show here, however, that although the conventional theory is of potential help in the 1980s, for other periods it fares badly. Especially intriguing is the recent experience, which will be the major focus of the new empirical work introduced in this chapter. The key message here is that, since 2000, even though the economy has experienced global shocks of the kind that might have been expected to increase wage inequality, wage inequality of the type predicted by theory has actually not increased. This observation suggests that the assumptions behind the application of the theory need to be reexamined.

Trade Theory

The workhorse Hecksher-Ohlin model of international trade forecasts that trade patterns will reflect endowments of factors of production. The model's predictions are clearest when there are two factors of production, in this case skilled and unskilled labor. Since skilled labor will be relatively abundant in developed countries, these countries will have a comparative advantage in skill-intensive products, and in autarky skill-intensive goods and services would be relatively cheap. Similarly, since unskilled labor would be relatively abundant in developing countries, their comparative advantage should lie in unskilled-labor-intensive products, and in autarky unskilled-labor-intensive goods will be relatively cheap. Opening up to trade will, therefore, lead developed countries to export skilled-labor-intensive products and import unskilled-labor-intensive products and lead developing countries to do the reverse.

It follows that opening up to trade will raise the relative price of skill-intensive goods and services in developed countries and the relative price of unskilled-labor-intensive goods and services in developing countries. These price changes provide the key link in this theory between trade and wages. Under competitive conditions, as shown by Wolfgang Stolper and Paul A. Samuelson (1941), an increase in the relative price of a good will raise the return to the factor of production used relatively intensively in its production and lower the return to the factor used less intensively.

Applying this theory to the United States could, in principle, help explain increased wage inequality since opening up to trade should raise the relative price of skilled-labor-intensive goods and services in the United States and boost skilled-labor wages and reduce unskilled-labor wages. Similar effects would be expected from trade liberalization in the United States and/or developing countries: Lower trade barriers in the United States will reduce the relative domestic price of unskilled-labor-intensive products that the United States imports and thus reduce the relative wages of unskilled US workers. Similarly, trade liberalization or uniform growth in the developing countries will raise the world (and US) relative price of skill-intensive products and thus also increase the return to skills and lower the return to unskilled labor in the United States.

The theory is based on the assumption that factors of production are completely mobile within each economy. This assumption means that in the long run, wage rates of workers with given skills must be the same throughout the entire economy. It is a very powerful assumption because it implies that even if only a small share of the economy participates directly in trade, the effects of trade will be felt throughout the entire economy, even in sectors producing goods and services that are not traded internationally.[1]

If the classical Stolper-Samuelson effects operate, then one would expect to see increased inequality along skill lines throughout the economy. It is also remarkable that this theory suggests "only traded goods (and services) prices matter." While changes in relative factor supplies will affect the composition of output, unless these are large enough to affect world prices, they will leave factor prices unaffected. This implication of the theory directly contradicts the huge body of work done by labor economists that tries to explain relative wages on the basis of changes in relative labor supplies within individual countries.

---

1. If factors are not internally mobile, however, then the effects of trade on wages could be felt only in the sectors to which the factors are confined. In this case, "specific" factors used in export sectors gain while those in import-competing sectors lose, and the degree and nature to which a sector is exposed to trade could matter. This is the so-called specific factors model of trade. For an exposition, see Krugman and Obstfeld (2000, chapter 3).

Conventional trade theorists have developed a second theory, which recognizes that all factors may not be mobile even in the long run. This "specific factors" model also predicts an association between trade and factor returns, with specific factors that are engaged in export industries benefiting and those in import-competing sectors losing. In this framework, the effects on mobile factors are ambiguous. While it would be of help in explaining increases in inequality that do not accord with general attributes (e.g., so-called within-cell inequality), it would not forecast strong effects in sectors that are not directly engaged in trade.

Another key assumption, which will be discussed further later, is that specialization is incomplete—i.e., both skilled- and unskilled-labor-intensive products are still produced in the United States. When specialization is incomplete, in fact, trade is a substitute for and replicates the international movement of factors of production. And under the assumption that technologies are similar worldwide, just as the free movement of workers would drive wages to equality, in this framework trade leads to global factor price equalization (Samuelson 1948). But trade and factor movements may not be complete substitutes if there is specialization. In this case, the connection between product and factor prices breaks down. Indeed under such circumstances, workers in the United States would be employed only in the skilled-labor-intensive sector, and their wages would be unaffected by drops in the relative price of the unskilled-labor-intensive product. In this case, domestic demand and relative factor supplies would influence factor prices.

Does this theory really do a good job in explaining increasing US wage inequality? The theory had some degree of success in the 1980s but does not work very well when the past quarter century is viewed as a whole. Judged either on the basis of quantity or price evidence, the correlation between increased trade and increased wage inequality is poor.

Timing of Wage Inequality

The previous chapter estimated that, between 1981 and 2006, wage inequality accounted for 6.8 log points of the gap between blue-collar product compensation and output per worker. This, in turn, was associated with a 12 percentage point decline in the compensation of blue-collar workers relative to white-collar workers. But the timing of the movement is noteworthy: 3.8 points of the 6.8-point gap occurred in the 1980s, 2.5 points in the 1990s, and just 0.4 points in the period since 2000.

Similarly, of the 12 percentage point decline in the ratio of blue-collar to white-collar compensation in the employment cost index (ECI), 9 percentage points took place between 1980 and 1990, 3 percentage points between 1990 and 2000, and none after 2000; and of the 25 percentage point rise in the college–high school premium, 15 percentage points took place in the 1980s and 10 percentage points in the 1990s, and none since 2000.[2] Thus, the story of wage inequality over the past quarter century is best told in three phases, and while reversals were rare, in each successive period, the increases in wage inequality were more moderate.

In the 1980s, pervasive increases in inequality are evident when workers are grouped by percentile, education, occupation, experience, and in the residuals that remain (so-called within-group inequality) once experience, education, and demographic characteristics are controlled for (Mishel, Bernstein, and Allegretto 2007, 141). In the 1990s, increasing wage inequality was more moderate and more subtle. Workers at the bottom of the earnings distribution were not particularly disadvantaged, and there were relatively smaller increases in within-cell inequality (Mishel, Bernstein, and Allegretto 2007, table 3.16, 141).

Comparing earnings in the 10th, 50th, and 90th percentiles captures the difference between the decades. In the 1980s, the story was inequality across the board, with the 50-10 and 90-50 ratios both increasing rapidly. But in the 1990s, the story is basically increased 90-50 inequality; if anything, the 50-10 gap has narrowed.[3] The 1990s issue is thus about the increases at the top end rather than inequality across the board.[4] Moreover, whether within-group inequality increased at all in the 1990s is still a matter of some controversy (Lemieux 2006). Strikingly, since the late 1990s, while there are additional increases in the 90-50 ratios (Goldin and Katz 2007), most other measures of wage inequality show little change.

Consider, for example, the occupational compensation series in the ECI reported in table 3.1. Between 1999 and 2005, nominal compensation for both blue- and white-collar workers increased by exactly the same amount—22 log points. This was also the case for the major upper-income occupational subcategories of management and professional workers as well as the major categories of blue-collar workers, both machine operators

---

2. US Census Bureau, table A.3 on Mean Earnings of Workers 18 Years and Over, by Educational Attainment, Race, Hispanic Origin, and Sex, available at www.census.gov/population.

3. According to Peter Gottschalk and Sheldon Danziger (2003), "wage growth during the recovery of the 90s was spread more evenly throughout the distribution than it was during the 1980s recovery. For females, the line is nearly flat, with wage growth between 10 and 15 percent for every point between the 10th and the 80th percentiles. For males, wages rose most at the bottom and at the top of the distribution—by 21 [percent] at the 5th percentile and by 27 percent at the 95th percentile. Wage growth was between 10 and 17 percent from the 10th through the 90th percentile."

4. The estimates of the highest wage earnings are problematic because the surveys that have been used for wage behavior have typically "top coded" earnings at the top of the income distribution. For confidentiality and other reasons, instead of explicitly entering the highest earnings, these earnings have simply been marked down as greater than a particular level, for example, $100,000. Since these levels have changed over time, it makes the data for the very highest wages especially unreliable.

Table 3.1 Employment cost index compensation, by occupation, December 1980–December 2006 (log scale, 2005 = 0)

Occupation	Employment share, 2002 (percent)	1980	1985	1990	1998	1999	2000	2005	2006
Private industry (all workers)	100	−1.02	−0.73	−0.52	−0.25	−0.22	−0.18	0	0.03
White-collar occupations	56	−1.07	−0.76	−0.54	−0.26	−0.22	−0.18	0	0.03
Management, business, and financial	15	n.a.	−0.76	−0.55	−0.27	−0.22	−0.18	0	0.03
Professional and related	16	n.a.	−0.76	−0.52	−0.25	−0.22	−0.18	0	0.04
Sales	12	n.a.	−0.70	−0.52	−0.23	−0.21	−0.16	0	0.02
Administrative support including clerical	13	n.a.	−0.77	−0.50	−0.25	−0.22	−0.18	0	0.03
Blue-collar occupations	30	−0.95	−0.69	−0.50	−0.25	−0.22	−0.18	0	0.03
Machine operators, assemblers, and inspectors		n.a.	−0.70	−0.50	−0.25	−0.22	−0.18	0	n.a.
Handlers and laborers		n.a.	−0.71	−0.52	−0.26	−0.22	−0.18	0	n.a.
Service occupations	14	−0.99	−0.68	−0.48	−0.23	0.20	−0.16	0	0.03

n.a. = not available

Source: Bureau of Labor Statistics, Employment Cost Index, available at www.bls.gov.

Table 3.2 Employment cost index compensation, by industry, December 1998–December 2006 (log scale, 2005 = 0)

Industry	1998	1999	2000	2005	2006
Goods	−0.27	−0.23	−0.19	0	0.03
Blue-collar goods	−0.26	−0.22	−0.18	0	0.03
Manufacturing	−0.27	−0.23	−0.19	0	0.02
Construction	−0.26	−0.22	−0.17	0	0.04
Services	−0.25	−0.22	−0.17	0	0.03
Blue-collar services	−0.25	−0.21	−0.18	0	0.03
Retail trade	−0.22	−0.19	−0.15	0	0.03
Wholesale trade	−0.25	−0.21	−0.17	0	0.03
Health services	−0.28	−0.25	−0.20	0	0.04
Educational services	−0.28	−0.25	−0.20	0	0.04
Finance, insurance, and real estate	−0.30	−0.26	−0.21	0	0.03
Union	−0.28	−0.25	−0.21	0	0.03
Blue-collar occupations	−0.28	−0.25	−0.21	0	0.03
Goods-producing	−0.29	−0.26	−0.21	0	0.02
Manufacturing	−0.29	−0.26	−0.22	0	0.01
Blue-collar manufacturing	−0.28	−0.25	−0.21	0	0.01
Service-providing occupations	−0.26	−0.24	−0.21	0	0.04
Nonunion	−0.25	−0.22	−0.17	0	0.03
Blue-collar occupations	−0.24	−0.20	−0.16	0	0.03
Goods-producing	−0.26	−0.23	−0.19	0	0.03
Manufacturing	−0.26	−0.22	−0.19	0	0.02
Blue-collar manufacturing	−0.24	−0.21	−0.17	0	0.03
Service-providing occupations	−0.25	−0.21	−0.17	0	0.03

Source: Bureau of Labor Statistics, Employment Cost Index, available at www.bls.gov.

and handlers and laborers. Only service occupations lagged behind, with increases of 2 percent less than the others.

The industry data in table 3.2 give a similar impression, with labor compensation in goods industries (up 23 log points) growing slightly faster than labor compensation in services industries (22 log points). Remarkably, given the major decline in manufacturing employment, manufacturing compensation growth was relatively strong. Even more remarkable, perhaps, given the widespread views that globalization has reduced worker bargaining power, was the very strong growth in the compensation of *unionized* workers in manufacturing—up 26 log points—although union members also did relatively better in service-providing industries.

Indeed, the raises received by blue-collar manufacturing workers were similar to those received by workers in health, education, and financial services—all of whom also enjoyed rapid increases. By contrast, perhaps because of a failure to raise minimum wages, the weakest wage performance was in retail trade—the quintessential nontraded goods sector.

Correlations Between Relative Wages and Prices

If the paradigm is that "only traded goods prices" matter, one should be able to correlate the movements of relative wages with price movements or with trade flows, which can be used as a proxy for price movements.[5] But as a review of the experience of the past 25 years suggests, the timing of wage inequality is not what might have been expected if increased trade penetration in the US economy always gives rise to increased wage inequality. To be sure, this evidence does not make it possible to rule out the possibility that these effects could operate with long and variable lags, with pressures from the 1970s leading to inequality in the 1980s and the effects of pressures after 2000 yet to come. But it would make for a rather complicated story that was more difficult to corroborate.

Between 1947 and 1970, the US economy remained fairly closed, with the sum of exports plus imports equal to around 10 percent of GDP. Over the 1970s, however, the share of trade in GDP doubled, reaching 20.6 percent of GDP by 1980. In part, this doubling reflected the impact of the two large oil price increases, which boosted US import costs and led to several dollar devaluations. These devaluations helped generate the export earnings required to pay for the imports. The price data for the 1970s also suggest increased global pressures. In the 1970s, according to Leamer (1998), relative prices of textiles and apparel—the paradigmatic unskilled-labor-intensive goods—fell by 30 percent (see also Baldwin and Cain 1997). Yet the 1970s were not a period with rising wage inequality. If anything college premiums fell, and toward the end of the decade wage growth was strong, particularly for unionized workers.

In the 1980s, even though the trade shares in GDP did not increase, the composition of imports changed significantly, as oil prices declined, and manufactured imports grew rapidly. Charting the ratio of exports plus nonoil imports suggests that the trend toward increased openness continued in the 1980s but still by not as much as in the 1970s (figure 1.4). Between 1980 and 1990, for example, the ratio of nonoil imports of goods to GDP increased from 6.1 to 7.5 percent. This growth in the 1980s was evenly split between imports from developing and developed countries. Imports from non-OPEC[6] developing countries increased from 2.2 to 2.8 percent of GDP, while imports from industrial countries increased from

---

5. Alan V. Deardorff and Robert W. Staiger (1988) give the justification for using the net factor content of trade as a proxy for price changes. See also Krugman (1995).

6. OPEC stands for Organization of Petroleum Exporting Countries.

Figure 3.1 Share of goods imports in US GDP, 1978–2006

percent

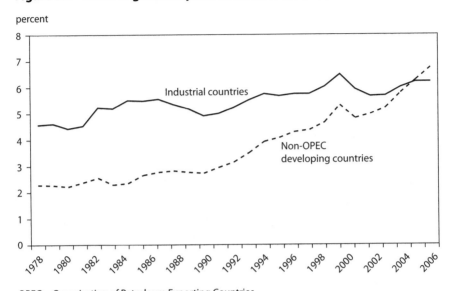

OPEC = Organization of Petroleum Exporting Countries

Source: Bureau of Economic Analysis, International Accounts Data, available at www.bea.gov.

4.6 to 5.2 percent (figure 3.1). While the import penetration growth in the 1980s was not insignificant, it was considerably smaller than in the 1970s or the 1990s.

For the 1980s, there is some dispute over the price evidence: Bhagwati (1991), Lawrence and Slaughter (1993), Leamer (1998), and Baldwin and Cain (1997) found little evidence that unskilled-labor-intensive products declined in relative prices. Jeffrey Sachs and Howard Shatz (1994) found some evidence but only after computer prices were dropped from their sample.[7] So in this period, virtually all measures of wage inequality show substantial increases but, compared with the 1970s or 1990s, the trade pressures appear to be relatively modest.[8] One would have to believe that there are substantial and variable time lags in the responses of wages to prices to claim that these data support the proposition that trade prices have significantly affected relative wages.

The 1990s were a second major period of increased opening, with imports of goods rising as a share of GDP from 8.6 to 12.5 percent. This rise was not as large as the increase in the 1970s, but this time the increase was concentrated in imports from developing countries. Non-OPEC merchan-

---

7. Feenstra and Hanson (1999) argue that because of outsourcing of intermediate inputs, data on final goods prices should not be the only focus of analysis. They find that offshoring did induce some increased wage inequality in the 1980s.

8. Slaughter (2000) provides an excellent summary.

Figure 3.2 Ratio of US nonagricultural export prices to prices of manufactured goods imports from industrial and developing countries, 1990–2006

log scale (2006 = 0)

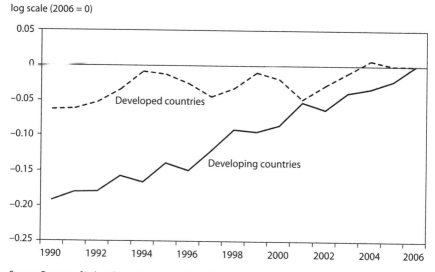

Source: Bureau of Labor Statistics, Import Price Data, available at www.bls.gov.

dise imports in the 1990s were up from 2.8 to 5.3 percent of US GDP, a rise that was almost double that of the growth in imports from industrial countries, which increased from 5.2 to 6.5 percent relative to GDP (figure 3.1).

What happened to prices during this period? The answers are mixed. Alan B. Krueger (1997) found that the relative prices of skill-intensive products increased between 1989 and 1994. Matthew J. Slaughter (2000) pointed out that his sample included only a third of manufacturing and found that when all manufacturing prices were sampled, Krueger's result was reversed. Over this period, wage inequality did continue to rise, though at a smaller pace than in the 1980s, and mainly due to rapid wage growth of the highest wage earners.

Since 1989, the Bureau of Labor Statistics (BLS) has reported separate import price data for manufactured goods the United States imports from developing and developed countries. The ratio of these prices could serve as a rough proxy for the relative price of unskilled-labor-intensive goods. A second proxy is to compare the prices of manufactured goods imported from developing countries to US nonagricultural export prices. As shown in figures 3.2 and 3.3, prices of manufactured goods from developing countries fell relative to both these measures. By contrast, US export prices and the prices of US manufactured imports from *developed* countries have moved at similar rates (figure 3.2). So this price evidence may be of some help in explaining some of the increased inequality of the 1990s. But it also

Figure 3.3 Ratio of prices of US manufactured goods imports from developing countries to prices of US manufactured goods imports from developed countries, 1990–2006

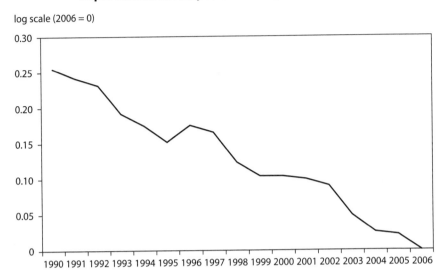

log scale (2006 = 0)

Source: Bureau of Labor Statistics, Import Price Data, available at www.bls.gov.

creates a puzzle for the period after 2000, in which wage inequality failed to show significant increases despite further declines in the relative prices of manufactured imports from developing countries.

After 2000, the share of imports from non-OPEC developing countries continued to grow rapidly, while the share of imports from developed countries actually declined (figure 3.1). By 2006, the value of imports from developing countries actually passed that of industrial countries. Yet this was a period of slow wage growth for almost all workers, with very little additional inequality (figures 3.4a, 3.4b, 3.5, and 3.6).

Controlling for Other Causes

Overall, there is an extremely weak correlation between import price pressures and increased wage inequality. But in any case, finding some association in timing between trade volumes and/or prices and relative wages would, of course, be only a starting point. The real challenge lies in coming up with more precise estimates of the effects of trade and in isolating, within a general equilibrium framework, the numerous other factors that could influence relative wages. These include technological change, relative supplies of skilled and unskilled workers, and changes in final product demand.

Figure 3.4a   Ratio of white- to blue-collar ECI compensation, 1981–2005

log scale (2005 = 0)

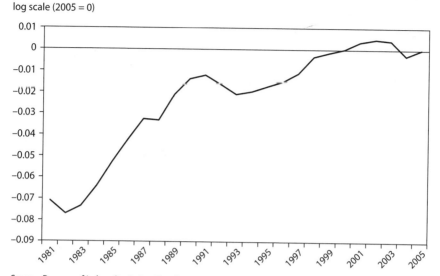

Source: Bureau of Labor Statistics, Employment Cost Index, available at www.bls.gov.

Figure 3.4b   Ratio of earnings of college graduates and advanced degree holders to earnings of high school graduates, 1975–2005

log scale (2005 = 0)

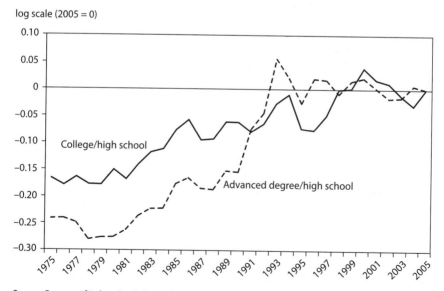

Source: Bureau of Labor Statistics and US Census Bureau, Current Population Survey, Educational Attainment data, available at www.census.gov.

Figure 3.5 Ratio of union to nonunion ECI compensation, 1980–2005

log scale (2005 = 0)

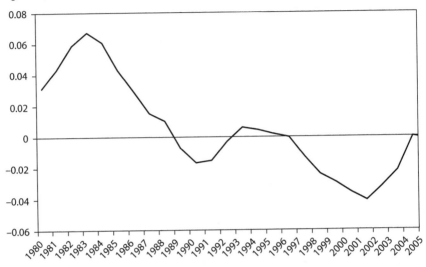

Source: Bureau of Labor Statistics, Employment Cost Index, available at www.bls.gov.

Three distinct approaches have been used. One is to measure the net factor content of trade (e.g., Borjas, Freeman, and Katz 1997); a second is to use econometric techniques to control for other variables and isolate the relative wage changes mandated by price changes (e.g., Harrigan 2000, Baldwin and Cain 1997); and a third is to use simulation models to explore the effects of reducing trade barriers (e.g., Cline 1997, Krugman 1995).

All three methods have been used to study wage inequality until the mid-1990s. Some studies do find some role for trade, but none claim it is the dominant reason for increased wage inequality. William Cline (1997, 144) provided an extensive summary of these studies and concluded that "a reasonable estimate based on the literature would be that international influences contributed about *20 percent* [italics added] of the rising wage inequality in the 1980s."[9] Most studies conclude that a much higher weight should be attributed to skill-biased technological change.[10]

My estimates suggested effects that are about half of those found by Cline in his literature review (Lawrence 1996, 69), but if I combine the estimate from chapter 2 that wage inequality accounts for 6.8 log points of the blue-collar wage-productivity gap with the estimates that "trade" ac-

9. In his own work based on simulations, Cline (1997, 144) himself concludes that "a *third* [italics added] of net increase in the skilled/unskilled ratio from 1973–93 was attributable to trade and an additional one-ninth was attributable to immigration." This attribution would mean that blue-collar wages might have been higher by 2.2 percent.

10. For an excellent summary, see Cline (1997, table 2.3).

Figure 3.6 Ratio of annual earnings of high school dropouts to high school graduates, 1975–2005

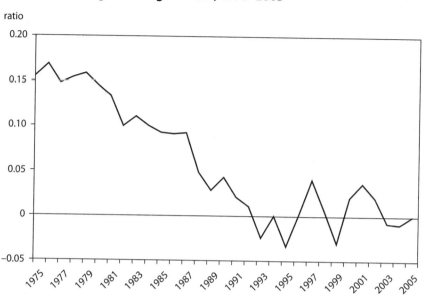

Source: Bureau of Labor Statistics and US Census Bureau, Current Population Survey, Educational Attainment data, available at www.census.gov.

counted for about 20 percent of the increased premium on skilled wages, I can conclude that *without the impact of trade on wage inequality between 1981 and 2006, the wages of blue-collar workers would have been 1.4 percent higher than they were in 2006 and that almost all of this took place before 2000.*

Paradox of Recent Wage Behavior

Given the trade pressures as indicated both by the price data going back to the early 1990s and the increased import penetration of goods and services from developing countries since 1993, two developments are noteworthy: first, the comparative stability of relative wages at broad skill levels since 1998 (figures 3.4a and 3.4b), and second, the stability of relative wages of the least educated workers since 1993 (indicated in figure 3.6 by the ratio of wages of high school dropouts to high school graduates). It seems reasonable to assume that imports from developing countries are particularly intensive in the use of unskilled workers and that their expansion would have a particularly adverse impact on the wages of the least skilled American workers. *Yet these workers have not fared particularly poorly.* But there is a way of explaining this outcome, and it suggests a surprising paradox. *Trade may cause less incremental inequality as it expands.*

In fact, Adrian Wood (1994) argued that the early effects of trade on the wages of unskilled workers were *larger* than most of the existing studies had implied because developed and developing countries actually produced different kinds of products. This meant that when studies used input-output coefficients taken from the developed countries, they were seriously underestimating the degree to which imports from developing countries used unskilled labor.[11] His view (Wood 1995) also led him presciently to reject the forecasts of those who argued that the impact of trade on the relative wages of unskilled workers in developed countries would become increasingly pronounced over time (e.g., Sachs and Shatz 1994, Krugman 2007).[12] Instead, he argued they would diminish.

The process Wood envisaged works like this: At the start, Stolper-Samuelson effects prevail because imports and domestic products are perfect substitutes, and the expansion of developing-country exports has adverse effects on the wages of unskilled workers in the United States. But over time, production of the most unskilled-labor-intensive products moves abroad, and eventually the US economy becomes fully specialized. Technically, the economy moves out of the cone of diversification and no longer produces unskilled-labor-intensive goods. The strong link between trade prices and factor prices is thus broken. If there are additional declines in the relative prices of imported unskilled-labor-intensive goods and services, US consumers gain, but US relative factor prices are unaffected.

This process of specialization could, of course, evolve, and over time the economy could become increasingly specialized as foreign countries increase the range of products in which they can compete. This, in turn, could eliminate additional US production.[13] Nonetheless, since the activities that are displaced are likely to be increasingly more skilled-labor-intensive, the impact of each additional expansion of trade on relative wage inequality diminishes since the ratio of skilled to unskilled workers who are displaced and have to be absorbed into the labor force increases. Thus, the marginal impact of increased offshoring, stressed by Robert C. Feenstra and Gordon H. Hanson (1999) for example, could well diminish over time as increasingly fewer unskilled-labor-intensive activities move abroad.

Another variant of adaptation to international competition is to produce the same products using different production techniques. A key assumption when applying the Stolper-Samuelson model is the absence of factor intensity reversals—i.e., one can talk of goods unambiguously as

---

11. For a critique of Wood, see Lawrence (1996).

12. Wood (1995, 77) wrote, "I do not expect unskilled workers in developed countries to be much hurt by even major new entry into the world market for low-skill intensive manufacturers, simply because these goods are no longer produced in developed countries. The entry of China and India, pushing down the world prices of these goods, will benefit developed-country workers, skilled and unskilled alike."

13. For a description of such a model involving offshoring, see Feenstra (2004, chapter 4).

skilled-labor and unskilled-labor-intensive. But it is possible that in the United States, firms could be driven by competition to use capital- and skilled-labor-intensive production methods to produce goods that abroad are produced using unskilled-labor-intensive methods. If this occurs, in the United States, increased competition from developing countries would not have a particularly adverse impact on unskilled labor.

A third possibility is that developing countries have upgraded the products they sell so that these products are now very similar to those produced in the United States. This could also be because, while some part of the production process is added in developing countries, much of the value is actually added in developed countries.[14] In addition to complete specialization, a considerable amount of trade also occurs *within* industries—so-called intraindustry trade—in which the United States imports and exports similar types of differentiated goods and services. The expansion of this type of trade too may not involve increased wage inequality because simultaneously imports and exports of the same kinds of products expand; even if imports do displace domestic goods and services, the skill-mix of the displacement could resemble that of the rest of the economy. In sum, complete specialization, factor intensity reversals, and upgrading and intraindustry trade could all result in the absence of a relationship between increased trade and inequality.

What Do the Data Tell Us?

Estimates at high levels of aggregation actually support the view that US imports are not intensive in unskilled labor. Indeed, they indicate that the United States imports goods that are produced in the United States by workers who, for the most part, earn wages that are considerably above the average. This view is compatible with the explanations that there have been factor reversals and/or that even developing countries now export relatively skill-intensive goods to the United States.

The BLS Occupational Employment Statistics (OES) survey reports the distribution of wages by industry.[15] For each industry, it provides wages at the 10th, 25th, 50th, 75th, and 90th percentiles of the wage distribution.[16] These wages have been matched and weighted using trade data by

---

14. Nicholas Lardy (2005, 132) reports, for example, that domestic value-added accounts for only 15 percent of the value of Chinese exported electronic and information technology products.

15. The OES survey provides earnings on an hourly and annual basis, including mean and median earnings for all areas—national, state, and metropolitan statistical areas—as well as 10th, 25th, 75th, and 90th percentile wage rate estimates for the nation. The survey is available at www.bls.gov/oes.

16. Wages for the OES survey are straight-time, gross pay, exclusive of premium pay.

Table 3.3 Hourly earnings distribution, 2005 (dollars per hour and ratio)

	Mean	10th percentile	25th percentile	Median	75th percentile	90th percentile
US manufacturing	18.87	8.70	11.07	15.31	22.43	33.62
US economy	18.21	7.26	9.46	14.15	22.2	33.74
Ratio to economywide distribution						
Manufacturing industries weighted by						
Exports	122	143	146	137	123	112
Imports	118	139	143	133	118	108
US manufacturing	104	120	117	108	101	100
US economy	100	100	100	100	100	100
Manufacturing weighted by						
2004 imports from Mexico	118	139	143	132	119	108
1997 imports from Mexico	117	139	142	130	117	106
2005 imports from China	114	128	129	124	115	108
1997 imports from China	100	118	114	105	97	94

Sources: US International Trade Commission Interactive Tariff and Trade Dataweb, available at http://dataweb.usitc.gov; Bureau of Labor Statistics, Occupational Employment Statistics, available at www.bls.gov/oes.

trade values that are available from 1997 through 2005. Data are reported for total US manufactured imports and exports as well as imports from China and Mexico. Also reported are the wage distributions for manufacturing as well as the entire US economy, again based on the OES. At the four-digit North American Industrial Classification System (NAICS) level of aggregation, the manufacturing sector is divided into 85 industries.

As reported in table 3.3, this exercise confirms that US international trade is concentrated in US manufacturing industries that pay high wages. In 2005, mean wages in manufacturing as a whole were 4 percent above the national average. However, four-digit NAICS industry average wages weighted by manufactured exports and imports were 22 and 18 percent above the national average, respectively. Mexican import-weighted wages matched those for manufacturing imports weighted by imports from all countries and were also 18 percent above the national average. Chinese 2005 import-weighted earnings were lower than manufactured imports in general but still 14 percent above the national average and 10 percent above the manufacturing average. The exercise also indicates that China has been upgrading its imports over time. Using 1997 Chinese import weights (and 2005 average earnings), I obtain mean wages of $18.20 per hour, basically equal to the national average wage of $18.21 per hour in

2005. This exercise suggests that if trade from any of these sources causes displacement, it is likely to be of workers with relatively high wages.

Exploring the wage distribution of these industries in greater detail is also illuminating. Table 3.3 indicates that manufacturing wages are not only higher on average than wages in the rest of the economy but also they are more concentrated in the middle of the earnings distribution. Workers at the bottom of the wage distribution in manufacturing earn substantially more than those in a similar position in the national distribution. Indeed, workers in the lowest 10th percentile in manufacturing earn 20 percent more than those in the 10th national percentile. This manufacturing premium declines monotonically as percentiles increase, with workers in the 90th percentile in manufacturing earning the same as those in the 90th percentile nationally.

An even stronger distributional pattern with these characteristics is evident with respect to manufactured goods that are exported or compete with imports. The 2005 export- and import-weighted earnings in the 10th percentile are 43 and 39 percent above the national average, respectively. The premium again diminishes in higher percentiles to 12 and 8 percent in the 90th percentile for exports and imports, respectively. This means that on average the US manufacturing workers employed in industries that are most engaged in international competition earn relatively high wages at all percentiles, with the highest percentage differences at the lowest percentiles. In 2005 the median US wage rate was $14.15 an hour. The wage distributions here suggest that almost 70 percent of all workers involved in exports or competing with imports earn wages that are above or at least close to the median level. All in all, therefore, this exercise confirms that when produced in the United States, the goods the United States imports pay relatively high wages to workers earning median wages or higher and US exports pay even higher wages.

Thus far, I have characterized the wage mix of employment in US industries, but what have been the effects of trade in changing that mix? Following the methodology of Baily and Lawrence (2004), I have undertaken an updated analysis that, taking productivity growth as given, allows me to attribute employment changes to changes in trade and domestic demand for three-digit NAICS industries between 2000 and 2005 using an input-output matrix. I then use the 2003 OES data to estimate the average wages and the distribution of wages of the jobs that were lost due to trade over this period.

Over this period, I find that the manufacturing jobs lost due to trade paid average wages that were 13.7 percent above the national average and 9 percent above the manufacturing average. A rough estimate suggests that two-thirds of the jobs lost due to trade paid more than the national average wage. Clearly, these numbers indicate that displacement due to trade should not be expected to exert a disproportionate downward influence on the relative wages of less-skilled workers and instead could, as suggested by Claudia Goldin and Lawrence Katz (2007) and Janet Yellen (2006), provide some of the explanation for the relatively weak performance of wages in the middle.

Nonetheless, while significant as a share of manufacturing employment, the scale is too small to exert a major impact on the aggregate wage structure. In the period 2000 to 2005, for example, my estimates using the input-output tables are that 1.3 million jobs in manufacturing were lost due to trade. So, about 1 million workers were displaced in a labor force of over 140 million (or 70 million between the 25th and 75th percentiles). Even if all these workers earned above the median wage, this impact is unlikely to have affected employment composition or wages in a major way.

A similar input-output analysis over a longer period has been undertaken by economists at the Economic Policy Institute, and it reaches very interesting conclusions (Mishel, Bernstein, and Allegretto 2007, table 3.30, 175). They estimate that total (not just manufacturing) job displacement due to trade between 2000 and 2004 was 1.9 million—about the same as the 1.8 million they estimate were displaced between 1979 and 1989. But the composition of displacement was very different. In particular, in the 1980s the job displacement was concentrated among less skilled workers: 12.2 percent of those displaced were college graduates, and 28 percent had less than high school education.

Similarly, 19.7 percent of the jobs lost were in wage percentiles above 75 percent of the national average, while 37.9 percent were in the lowest quintile. But displacement since 2000 was very different: 21.3 percent of the displaced were college graduates, 31.9 percent in jobs that would have fallen above the 75th wage percentile, and just 14.2 percent in the lowest quintile. Particularly noteworthy is that the composition of the displacement is remarkably similar to the overall composition of employment.

In the 1980s, therefore, it was possible, using input-output analysis and other data at fairly high levels of aggregation, to detect trade displacement of skilled and unskilled workers in proportions that were different from the labor force in general. In particular, displacement due to trade was relatively concentrated among unskilled workers, which led to numerous studies that argued that trade had contributed to wage inequality (e.g., Sachs and Shatz 1994; Borjas, Freeman, and Katz 1997). But in the 1990s and after 2000, this has not been the case. Using US input-output coefficients, the net factor content of trade looks increasingly like the factor content of the US economy in general.

Nonetheless, there is also evidence that by undertaking the analysis at high levels of aggregations (such as three-digit NAICS, which divides manufacturing into 20 industries, and four-digit NAICS, which has 85 industries), one could miss some part of the story. The Wood critique may be relevant. If many of the products imported from developing countries are no longer produced in the United States, it is an error to use US input-output coefficients to measure the factor content of US trade.

Indeed, there is empirical support for the view that many of the products imported from developing countries, for example, are qualitatively different from those made in the United States or imported from developed countries. Peter Schott (2004), for example, has studied highly disaggregated unit value data and concluded that while the United States increasingly sources the products with the same name (or in the same classification category) from both high- and low-wage countries, the unit values within products varied systematically with exporter relative factor endowments and exporter production techniques. He concludes, "These facts reject factor proportions specialization across products but are consistent with such specialization within products."

Similarly Andrew Bernard, Bradford Jensen, and Peter Schott (2006) show how US firms are able to survive in labor-intensive sectors by adopting more capital-intensive methods and using more technologically sophisticated production techniques. Thus, both the notion of complete specialization and the ideas of factor-intensity reversals are apparent in the disaggregated data.

The following analysis supports the idea that a more nuanced picture would emerge at more disaggregated levels of data collection (table 3.4). I have collected data from 385 six-digit industries from the 2002 Census and matching trade values for 2006 and 1997. These data do not give the wage distributions in each industry but do report payrolls and employment. Accordingly, the average wage for each industry was calculated for 2002, and the industries were then ranked by average wage. In 2002 the median manufacturing industry wage was $15.69 per hour, and the average wage in manufacturing was $16.55. When the six-digit industry average wages are weighted by 2006 import shares, the result is an average wage of $19.72—19 percent above the manufacturing average.

This result again suggests that manufactured imports into the United States are skewed toward industries paying relatively high wages. This might have been expected for imports from *developed* countries and, in fact, using the shares of imports from developed countries as weights produces an average wage of $21.35—29 percent above the manufacturing average in 2006. Even using the weighted average of import shares from developing countries produces an average wage of $17.42—5 percent higher than the $16.55 average for manufacturing. Weighting by the 2006 shares of imports from China, however, yields an average of $15.14, which is still 9 percent lower than the manufacturing average. So in contrast to the more aggregated estimates, at this more disaggregated level, it does appear that imports from China in 2006 are still in relatively low-wage industries, but this is not the case for manufactured goods from developing countries as a whole.

It is also evident that imports from all sources are increasing relatively rapidly in higher-wage sectors, since in all cases using 2006 imports as weights produces higher averages than using 1997 shares as weights. The

Table 3.4 Distribution of production worker average hourly wages in US manufacturing industries (six-digit NAICS industries), 2002
(dollars per hour and ratio)

Industry	25th percentile	50th percentile	75th percentile	90th percentile	Mean
US manufacturing	13.52	15.69	19.60	23.00	16.55
Industry average earnings weighted by					
1997 imports	13.55	18.38	22.62	32.11	19.35
2006 imports	13.67	19.06	23.59	32.11	19.72
Imports from developed countries					
1997	15.48	20.06	24.11	33.15	20.77
2006	15.64	20.10	24.73	33.15	21.35
Imports from developing countries					
1997	11.31	14.00	20.55	23.62	16.37
2006	12.53	15.57	20.55	28.07	17.42
Imports from China					
1997	9.95	12.68	14.67	19.52	13.28
2006	12.49	13.47	19.08	20.55	15.14
Ratio to US manufacturing					
1997 imports	100	117	115	140	117
2006 imports	101	121	120	140	119
Imports from developed countries					
1997	114	128	123	144	125
2006	116	128	126	144	129
Imports from developing countries					
1997	84	89	105	103	99
2006	93	99	105	122	105
Imports from China					
1997	74	81	75	85	80
2006	92	86	97	89	91

NAICS = North American Industrial Classification System

Sources: US Census Bureau; US International Trade Commission Interactive Tariff and Trade Dataweb, available at http://dataweb.usitc.gov.

acceleration has been largest in the case of China, up from 80 percent using 1997 import weights to 91 percent of the manufacturing average using 2006 import weights. It is also evident in the case of imports from all developing countries—up from 0.99 to 1.05 percent of average US wages—and from developed countries—up from 1.25 to 1.27.[17]

---

17. Dani Rodrik (2006) reports that Chinese exports are more advanced than would be expected from the Chinese level of GDP per capita.

All in all, the analysis suggests that overall, imports into the United States compete with US industries paying higher than average wages and that imports from all sources have become increasingly sophisticated. The evidence confirms that the United States has responded in part to import competition from developing countries either by no longer producing unskilled-labor-intensive goods and services or by adopting more skill-intensive production methods. At the same time, the manufactured goods the United States imports from both developed and especially developing countries have become more sophisticated. The result is that imported products are not particularly relatively intensive in unskilled labor when produced in the United States. This means that lower imported prices of goods from developing countries do not generally increase US wage inequality because either they simply provide benefits to US consumers or they displace US workers with skills that are similar to those in the rest of the workforce.

This analysis not only helps to explain why the rapid import penetration by developing countries has not been associated with unusually weak wages among the least skilled Americans but also suggests that, unlike the earlier period, trade has not been reinforcing the effects of immigration on these workers' wages. Most immigrants to the United States have less than a high school education and earn significantly less than the median wage distribution.

As noted by George Borjas (2003), according to the 2000 Census, 32 percent of the immigrant population had not completed 12 years of schooling compared with just 11 percent of the native population. Borjas also estimates that immigrants comprise around 25 percent of the workers in each of the bottom two deciles. It is still possible, ceteris paribus, that immigration exerts downward pressure on the relative wages of unskilled workers, but if immigration was having a *dominant* impact, it should show up primarily in the gap between the relatively unskilled and the most unskilled workers—i.e., between high school and less than high school—and in the 50-10 ratio widening. The declining inequality in the 1990s with respect to the earnings of the poorest workers is particularly noteworthy, therefore, both for those concerned with immigration and about import competition from developing countries.

The discussion in this chapter mirrors a similar debate among labor economists. As time has gone on, it appears that simplistic applications of the technology explanation for inequality have run into trouble because skill premiums have not changed in the manner that might have been predicted. As the new patterns have emerged, some labor economists have increasingly begun to question or refine the role that skill-biased technological change has played.[18]

---

18. Lawrence Mishel and Jared Bernstein (1998) were prescient early skeptics.

In particular, David Card and John E. DiNardo (2002) undertake numerous tests, all of which suggest that the connection between the spread of information technology and wage inequality is weak. They demonstrate that the timing of the growth in wage inequality is hard to reconcile with skill-biased technological change and emphasize the role of the failure to raise minimum wages in the early 1980s. Thomas Lemieux (2006) similarly finds that "the growth in both residual and between group wage inequality is all concentrated in the 1980s" and questions the idea of a trend movement in skill-biased technological change.

David Autor, Lawrence Katz, and Melissa Kearney (2005, 2006), however, emphasize the continuation of increased inequality at the top of the wage distribution in the 1990s and the relative decline in both the number of jobs and wages in the middle of the income distribution. They develop a new theory of skill-biased technological change in which computers complement nonroutine cognitive tasks and substitute for routine tasks but have little effect on manual tasks found at the bottom. The result is downward pressure on wages and employment opportunities for workers in the middle.

Both Goldin and Katz (2007) and Yellen (2006) argue that the globalization of production has similar properties in inducing polarization of wage distribution. They suggest that suppliers of personal services at the low end escape downward pressures from trade because these services must be provided locally. However, trade rewards those at the top while offshoring hurts those in the middle.

The analysis here did confirm that the industries involved in US manufacturing trade, both those competing with imports and those producing exports, employ a disproportionate number of people earning middle-income wages. It is less clear, however, whether offshored services, many of which involve business process outsourcing of low-skilled jobs for call centers and data processing, share the characteristic of being intensive in middle-income jobs, and while the effect of manufacturing displacement due to trade does go in the right direction, it does not appear that the scale of the displacement due to imports has been sufficiently large for offshoring to be a major part of the polarization story.

4

Class Inequality and Trade

It seems fair to say that America is driven more by greed than envy. Americans appear to have a considerable tolerance for income inequality in part because they believe, notwithstanding evidence to the contrary, that the US economy provides for a considerable amount of mobility and those who are poor today will be rich tomorrow. In addition, according to Edward Glaeser, the failure of the welfare state in the United States to expand to the degree it has in Europe is attributable to America's political institutions and its ethnic diversity (Glaeser 2005, Alesina and Glaeser 2004). Nonetheless, Americans do care deeply about their own economic well being, and in this respect, for most of them, the period between 2000 and 2006 has been deeply disappointing.

As measured by the employment cost index of the Bureau of Labor Statistics, private real wages and real compensation are up by just 2.1 and 5.6 percent, respectively. Particularly striking has been the fact that the average wage growth of workers at all but the very highest levels of skill and education has been equally poor. For most blue-collar workers, the recent weak wage growth continued a longer-run trend of slow real wage increases, which had been interrupted by the second half of the 1990s, but for workers with a college education, the recent slow real wage growth is a relatively new experience because these workers had seen their real pay rise steadily between 1980 and 2000. It is, therefore, not surprising that real wages and incomes have become a matter of concern.

Between 2000 and 2006, the big inequality story in the United States is the shift in income shares from labor to capital. The estimates derived in chapter 2 suggest that had income gains between 2000 and 2006 been divided in proportion to shares in 2000, real compensation of blue-collar workers, which actually increased by 4.9 percent, would have been higher by another 5.2 percent. Given that white-collar compensation increased at

**Figure 4.1   Share of labor compensation in US national income,
1947–2006**

percent

Source: Bureau of Economic Analysis, National Income and Product Accounts, table 1.12, available at www.bea.gov.

about the same pace as blue-collar compensation—by 5.4 percent—a roughly similar improvement would have occurred in white-collar compensation. The aggregate data from the 2001–06 period are certainly compatible with the view that global forces have induced a structural change in the income shares of labor and capital. But there are also reasons to be skeptical that this structural change reflects such forces.

First, while the US economy has been globalizing for a long time, unlike many other countries, the share of labor compensation in national income in the United States has been relatively stable (figure 4.1).[1] After rising steadily between 1950 and the late 1960s, the share has basically fluctuated within a fairly narrow range of around 66 percent (averaging 65.6 percent between 1970 and 1999). Globalization in the United States increased most dramatically over the 1970s—the years in which labor's share in income *increased* significantly, and taking the period 1970 through 2006 as a whole, there is no evidence of a major trend in either direction.[2]

---

1. Ian Dew-Becker and Robert Gordon (2005) and Anne E. Harrison (2002) reach a similar conclusion.

2. The long-run trends in labor's share in other industrial countries are very mixed, and perceived trends are sensitive to the period that is examined. Dirk Schumacher, Jan Hatzius, and Tetsufumi Yamakawa (2007) find evidence of falling labor shares in incomes in Germany

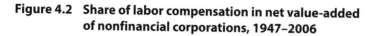

Figure 4.2   Share of labor compensation in net value-added of nonfinancial corporations, 1947–2006

percent

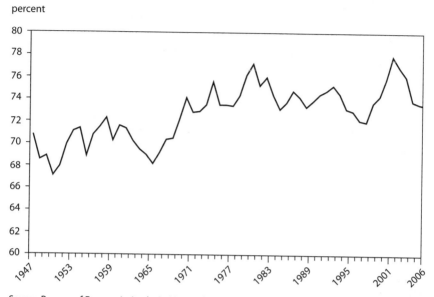

Source: Bureau of Economic Analysis, National Income and Product Accounts, table 1.14, available at www.bea.gov.

It is only in the period since 2000 that labor's share has declined: In 2006 the compensation share was relatively low—63.9 percent—about 2.2 percent below its peak share in 2001 and 1.6 percent below the long-run average but about the same share as in 1997.[3] Focusing more narrowly on the nonfinancial business sector provides a similar picture. In 2006 labor's share of 73 percent of net value-added was considerably below its peak in 2001 (77.4 percent) but above levels recorded in 1997 (71.5 percent), 1988 (72.8 percent), and 1984 (72.6 percent) (figure 4.2).[4]

If global forces are responsible for the recent shift in income shares, the character of recent wage pressures has to be very different from that prevailing earlier. One possibility is that recent wage behavior differs because

and Japan but not in France or Italy. Harrison (2002) reports that labor shares increased in Japan, Canada, and Switzerland, but shares declined in many other European countries. See also IMF (2007). Olivier J. Blanchard (1998) emphasizes that declining shares in Europe are in part a reaction to rising shares in the 1970s. He ascribes the declining share of labor after 1980 to shifts in the distribution of rents away from workers and to the use of technologies biased against labor. See also Guscina (2007) for a statistical analysis of changes in labor's share of income using an international sample.

3. In the first half of 2007, the share increased to 64.5 percent.

4. The share increased to 74 percent in the first half of 2007.

trade pressures have expanded up to higher levels of the wage distribution. Indeed, this view is compatible with some of the evidence introduced in the previous chapter although it raises the question of why wage growth was relatively strong in the latter 1990s despite similar trade pressures.

One source recently could be the India effect: While earlier trade pressures affected only unskilled workers, trade now puts downward pressures on the earnings of all kinds of workers because of the increased ability to offshore services electronically. But as discussed in greater depth in chapter 5, the evidence is that while they have grown rapidly, the scale of offshored activities is too small to have already had such a significant impact (Baily and Lawrence 2004). To be sure, the potential threat of outsourcing could reduce wages, but again this threat is likely to be plausible thus far only for a limited number of occupations such as software programmers and not for most workers.[5]

A second source that could be boosting profits is the China effect: the increased ability to offshore manufacturing production (Shelburne 2004). While China has been growing rapidly since the early 1980s, it is possible that the magnitude of its engagement has reached levels that now make it a significant factor in US wage determination. There is some evidence that between 1999 and 2004, US multinational firms have been expanding their employment shares in their foreign affiliates.

In contrast to the experience of the 1990s, when parent employment actually increased more rapidly than employment in foreign affiliates, since 1999, employment in US parents has been declining, while affiliate employment has been growing. But the recent employment pattern in US multinational corporations actually reflects developments outside of manufacturing, in industries such as wholesale and retail trade in which offshoring is not likely to be a major factor (Mataloni and Yorgas 2006). The data indicate that US firms have increased their overseas operations but more to service the nontraded parts of the foreign economies rather than to source traded goods abroad.

More generally, if increased offshoring is responsible for depressing the share of compensation, one would expect to see these pressures operating particularly strongly in the tradable goods sectors. The share of compensation should have been especially depressed in manufacturing, for example. But this has not been the case. In 2005, for example, the ratio of the share of compensation in manufacturing to the share in services was the same as in 2000. In addition, one might have expected these pressures to be operating by weakening the bargaining power of organized labor in manufacturing—yet compensation of unionized workers, especially those in manufacturing, has grown relatively rapidly during this period (figure

---

5. There is, in fact, evidence that wages and employment of software programmers have both declined since 2000, but it is hard to separate the impact of offshoring from that of the bursting of the internet bubble. See Mann (2006).

3.5). Instead it has been the financial sector in which profit shares have been growing particularly rapidly and in which labor's share stands at historic lows.[6]

It is likely, therefore, that a significant proportion of the low compensation share is cyclical. Profits are far more volatile than wages, and the share of labor fluctuates over the cycle, although not in a manner that is precisely pro- or anticyclical. Instead, labor's share is at its highest in the more mature phase of expansions and at the start of recessions; while labor's share falls as the recovery sets in, productivity accelerates and profits surge. By contrast, profit shares are highest in the middle of expansions and fall as the expansion matures and wage pressures build up.

As shown in figure 4.1, this was clearly what happened in the expansion from 1992 through 2000, in which labor's share fell from 65.9 percent in 1992 to 63.9 percent in 1997 before returning to a peak of 66.2 percent in 2001. Thus, the experience between 2001 and 2006 is quite similar in magnitude and phasing to that between 1992 and 1997, and if the past is prologue, labor's prospects should improve as the current expansion matures. If labor returned to its more typical share of 66 percent, compensation would be 2/66—i.e., 3 percent higher than in 2006. This number would be a reasonable estimate of the impact of the current cycle on earnings.

Part of the disgruntlement of US workers recently is that more of their compensation has come in the form of benefits due to rising health care costs and less in the form of wages. As indicated in figure 4.3, this rise is a marked change from the 1995–2000 period, when benefit costs actually declined as a share of income. The strong growth of compensation among unionized workers is not due to strong wage growth but to the fact that health care benefits have become more costly.

Finally, it should be noted that the strength of corporate profits since 2001 does not just reflect weak compensation. The 4 percent rise in the share of corporate profits in national income between 2000 and 2006 is far greater than the decline in the share of compensation (2.2 percent). This rise in corporate profits has been possible because of large declines in the share of net interest payments (1.9 percent) and rental incomes (1 percent).

So a sizable share of the redistribution recently has actually taken place among capitalists rather than between capital and labor as well as toward the financial sector. Unusually low interest rates, which were a characteristic of the 2001–06 expansion, have particularly affected this redistribution.

In sum, American workers of all skill levels are understandably concerned about their slow income growth, and the idea that global wage arbitrage has been exerting downward pressure on income growth is certainly plausible. But the sectoral patterns are not compatible with this

---

6. Profits in financial corporations accounted for 29 percent of all profits in 2000 but 46 percent of the growth between 2000 and 2006 (Bureau of Economic Analysis, National Income and Products Accounts, table 1.14).

Figure 4.3   Share of benefits in US national income, 1980–2006

percent

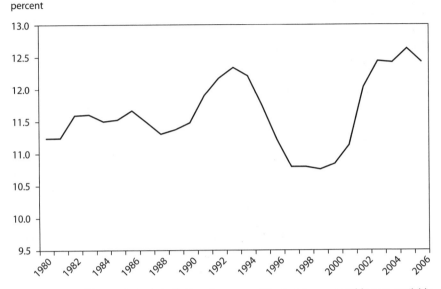

Source: Bureau of Economic Analysis, National Income and Product Accounts, table 1.12, available at www.bea.gov.

interpretation. Since there are reasons to believe the depressed share of labor compensation has a strong cyclical component, before concluding that this force has been the principal reason for wages lagging behind productivity growth, it will be necessary to see what happens as this expansion matures and the labor market tightens.

5

Globalization, Stock Options, and the Super Rich

In this chapter, I consider the role trade might have played in the rapid increase in the wage incomes of the richest Americans—i.e., those in the top 1 and one-tenth of 1 percent. This category includes a fairly wide range of occupations, but one group that has received considerable attention is the highest paid business executives. Accordingly, I first consider their pay. I point to the close correspondence between their wage increases and the rise in stock market prices. I then explore two contrasting explanations for this association. The first emphasizes power relations and the ability of executives to extract rents from shareholders. The second emphasizes market forces and rational efficiency and incentive considerations.

Since US multinational corporations were as reliant on the domestic market in 2000 as they were in 1980, I argue that both the power and market-based explanations imply that domestic developments rather than international trade are the dominant source of soaring chief executive officer (CEO) pay. I also briefly consider the role of trade in the increased earnings of other "superstars" and wealthy individuals and again suggest that for the most part, these increased fortunes were predominantly made in the United States. While globalization has increased the scale of the markets in which these individuals can compete, the driving forces behind the incomes at the top lie elsewhere.

In chapter 2, I concluded that in 2006, blue-collar wages would have been higher by 3.1 percent had the additional wage increases between 1981 and 2006 that are not captured in the employment cost index (ECI) been distributed proportionately to all workers. I called these "increases to the super rich," but the estimates were obtained as a residual between the broadest aggregate average hourly compensation measure and the labor compensation components based on ECI data that I could attribute to other causes. In that data, almost the entire shortfall is attributable to developments after 1990 and occurred particularly in the late 1990s.

This timing—with a negative residual in the mid-1990s and positive residual at the end of the decade—is consistent with the increased use of nonqualified stock options, which are treated as wage income but only when exercised. The shortfall in the mid-1990s could indicate options that were granted but not yet recorded as wages, and the positive residual later could indicate realizations made during the stock market boom in the late 1990s. Nonetheless, the residual could also reflect increases in other wage earnings at the very top, which are not captured in the ECI, and to stock option realizations by workers with wages that are less than those in the top 1 percent of the wage distribution.

Because they use a different methodology, Social Security returns data can be used to check the assertion that the residual captures gains at the very top.[1] In 1990, the top 1 percent of Social Security returns accounted for 11 percent of all wage incomes.[2] By 2000 that share rose to 13.9 percent, and, while it fell during the recession and stock market slump in 2001, the share increased again and stood at 13.3 percent in 2005.[3] This rise in the share of the top 1 percent between 1990 and 2003, if distributed evenly, would have been sufficient to increase wages of all other workers by 2.7 percent (2.3/86.7), which is not all that different from the 3.1 percent estimate obtained by quite different methods referred to above or the estimate for the same period obtained using the tax data provided by Emmanuel Saez and Thomas Piketty.[4]

In fact, a focus on the top 1 percent—a group of about 1.5 million wage earners—obscures the degree to which earnings have become even more concentrated, because most of the rise in the share actually occurred in the

---

1. The Social Security data are readily available only after 1990. These data are different from those on average hourly earnings for three reasons: First, they include wage earnings outside the business sector; second, they indicate annual rather than hourly earnings and will be affected by hours worked; and third, they exclude benefits, which are part of compensation but not subject to Social Security taxes. These data are available at www.ssa.gov.

2. The numbers are reported in discrete categories. I assume that the distribution is even across each category where the categories do not correspond to the required percentiles. I also make no effort to adjust the highest category. For example, the top category in 2005 is for wages of $50 million or above, and all earnings in this category are assumed to equal $50 million, thereby understating the likely share of wages at the very top.

3. In 1990, to qualify for the top 1 percent of Social Security returns, wages earnings had to be over $100,000. By 2000, this benchmark had increased to $175,000, and by 2005, it stood at $200,000.

4. These income tax statistics are available on their website at http://elsa.berkeley.edu /~saez.

very top one-tenth of 1 percent.[5] A rough estimate is that fully 2 of the 2.3 percentage point increase of the top 1 percent between 1990 and 2005 came in the earnings of the top one-tenth of 1 percent—which numbers just 155,000 Americans with wage income starting at around $750,000 in 2000.[6] From the perspective of this study, the question is why this has happened and in particular whether international trade has played an important role in it.

Top Executives

One group at the top whose pay has attracted particular attention is CEOs. Ian Dew-Becker and Robert J. Gordon (2005), for example, argue that CEOs and other top executives account for a significant share of the very top wage earners.

As computed by the AFL-CIO, in 1980 the ratio of average CEO earnings to the pay of the average worker was 42. By 1990 it had risen to 107 and by 2000 to an astounding 525. In 2005 it stood at 412. Overall, the 12.5-fold increase in the ratio over the two decades is remarkably similar to the 12-fold rise in Standard & Poor's (S&P) stock market index between 1980 and 2000.[7] Indeed, Brian Hall and Kevin J. Murphy (2003) produce a chart in which a measure of the ratio of the average CEO total pay to the average hourly annual earnings of production workers tracks the Dow Jones industrial average with remarkable precision over an even longer period from 1970 to 2002.

The fact that CEO pay tracks the stock market is perhaps not surprising given the increased use of stock options in their pay. Hall and Murphy (2003) report that as recently as 1992, stock options were not particularly common as a means of compensation. In 1992, for example, firms making up the S&P 500 granted their employees stock options with a total value of $11 billion (2002 dollars). By 2000, however, these same firms' grants had increased to $119 billion (2002 dollars). Tax law changes passed in 1994 were important in generating this increased use of options. In section

---

5. In 1990 earnings in this group in the Social Security data started at just over $350,000, and their share accounted for 3.6 percent. By 2000, the threshold was $750,000, and the share was 5.8 percent. In 2005 that group's share was slightly lower at 5.6 percent.

6. Between 1990 and 2005, the tax wage data show an increase in the share of the top 1 percent of 2.63 percent (versus the 2.3 percent obtained above from the Social Security data). Similarly, the rise in the share of the top one-tenth of 1 percent is 1.75 percent in the income tax data versus 2 percent in the Social Security data. See the Saez and Piketty income tax statistics at http://elsa.berkeley.edu/~saez.

7. The S&P index increased from 119 in 1980 to 1427 in 2000 (Council of Economic Advisers, *Economic Report to the President 2006*, February, 393).

162 (m) of the Internal Revenue Code, Congress had denied firms the ability to take tax deductions for compensation of top executives in excess of $1 million. At the same time, however, perhaps reflecting academic views that CEO pay and firm performance were poorly aligned, it allowed full deduction of "performance-based compensation," including payments from exercising options.[8]

The use of options for compensation was especially prevalent in industries in the "new economy," such as computers, software, and the internet. Stock options also became increasingly common as a means of compensating employees other than top executives, in part because their use allowed firms to share both the risks and rewards with their employees.[9] As the stock market boomed in the late 1990s, it is not surprising that CEO pay increased in tandem.

Why Has the Top Done So Well?

The fact that the increased earnings of top executives have been heavily concentrated in stock options does not deal with the more basic question of why their earnings, in whatever form, have been rising so rapidly. The literature on this question reflects a heated debate over whether top executives have done so well because they have simply become more skillful at "skimming" more from their stockholders or whether their pay is an accurate reflection of the increased value of their performance (i.e., marginal product) and results from an arm's-length market process. Lucian Bebchuk and Jesse Fried (2003) characterize the former as "the managerial power approach" and the latter as "the optimal contracting approach." They identify with the managerial power view and argue that there are problems with the optimal contracting approach.

In empirical work, Bebchuk and Yaniv Grinstein (2005) suggest that fundamentals such as increasing firm size, rate of return, or the growth in the rate of return cannot explain the rise in CEO pay. Others, such as Dew-Becker and Gordon (2005), who also argue that there are agency problems, point to CEO pay differences between the United States and other countries as evidence that something more than CEO marginal product seems to be at work (Abowd and Bognonno 1995, Conyon and Murphy 2000, Bloom and Van Reenen 2007). Instead, Bebchuk and Grinstein (2005) suggest that the only real limit to US managerial rent extraction is an "outrage

---

8. See Jensen and Murphy (1990). But see also Hall and Liebman (1998) for a refutation of this view.

9. In fact, the vast majority of options, about 90 percent of those granted in S&P 500 firms in 2002 were held by employees at levels below the top 5, but many of these, when exercised, would have been mostly subject to capital gains taxes rather than treated as regular wage income.

constraint," which was weakened because rising stock prices made investors more accepting of high CEO pay. They also note that institutional investors and others appear to have been persuaded that incentive-based pay was appropriate, and this made it easier to raise CEO pay through options rather than cash payments. Dew-Becker and Gordon (2005) offer, in a similar vein, what they call "the scratch my back model," which involves CEOs colluding with the committees that are responsible for setting their pay.[10] And Hall and Murphy (2003) suggest that when granting pay in the form of stock options, these committees were confused by accounting practices about their true worth.

There is, however, a view that CEO pay can be explained by economic fundamentals and not by accidents or unique historic or institutional developments. Xavier Gabaix and Augustin Landier (2006) develop an ingenious model in which CEO compensation is directly related to firm size in theory, and they then verify that the model works well empirically. They show how the increased market value of firms combined with small differences in CEO talent could result in the very large pay differences that match the market value increases that have taken place. They state, "The six-fold increase of CEO pay between 1980 and 2003 can be fully attributed to the six-fold increase in market capitalization of large US companies during that period." Their argument rests on the insight that the decisions made by CEOs of firms operating on a very large scale are highly consequential. Accordingly, the largest firms will pay very high premiums to ensure that the very best people make these decisions, even if the difference between the very best and the second best is relatively small. Gabaix and Landier also argue that institutional and cultural factors are not required to explain why US CEOs earn more than their foreign counterparts. Recognizing the large size of US firms and making the assumption that the markets for CEOs are still basically national suffice to account for the differences.[11]

Both these approaches appear to have valid elements. On the one hand, it does seem to be the case that over the past few decades, CEO pay has become more closely tied to stock market performance, suggesting an institutional evolution and arrangements that were not always based on a single model.[12] One the other, there is considerable evidence that these pay arrangements do have a rational, economically sound basis that can be explained by conventional economic theory.

What do these competing perspectives imply for the role of trade in particular or globalization generally in this type of income inequality? Does it make a difference which view is preponderantly correct? The market

---

10. Hall and Murphy (2003) are more skeptical. In particular, they point out that boards have become more independent, and options actually have become more transparent.

11. Dew-Becker and Gordon (2007) critique and challenge these empirical results.

12. This is confirmed by Hall and Liebman (1998), Dew-Becker and Gordon (2007), and Frydman and Saks (2007).

Table 5.1 Share of US parents of majority-owned foreign affiliates (MOFAs) in overall multinational activity

Year	Total	Parents	Parent share (percent)	MOFA share (percent)
Value-added (billions of dollars)				
1982	1,019.73	796.01	78	22
1990	1,364.88	1,044.88	77	23
2000	2,748.11	2,141.48	78	22
2004	3,040.14	2,215.80	73	27
Employment (millions)				
1982	23.73	18.71	79	21
1990	23.79	18.43	77	23
2000	32.06	23.89	75	25
2004	30.00	21.38	71	29

Source: Mataloni and Yorgas (2006).

power approach points to features of US corporate governance that generally have little to do with international trade or globalization. Instead, they reflect legal and institutional developments that are fundamentally domestic in character. Some proponents of the market power view do argue that rising stock markets in the 1990s and the use of stock options made it easier for top executives to obtain their gains, but only in as much as asset values have reflected international trade would it be given an explicit part in the story. The second line of explanation emphasizing market fundamentals places firm value and market size at the heart of the story.[13] In this framework, if globalization leads US firms to become larger, it could play a more central role in raising the demand for those with the skills to become CEOs.

Thus, from both perspectives a key question seems to be whether globalization has actually increased the size and value of US firms in the period when CEO earnings have accelerated. Many of the largest US firms are multinational, and it is plausible, as Yellen (2006) suggests, that this is the case.

Data on US multinational corporations help answer this question. And they yield a very surprising result. On average, US multinational firms were basically no more globalized in 2000 than they were in 1980! In 2000, for example, the operations of majority-owned foreign affiliates (MOFAs)

---

13. "Our theory predicts that the average CEO compensation . . . should change in proportion to the average size of firms in that group, to the power alpha. The prior section concluded that the US 1992–2004 panel evidence was consistent with alpha = 1, i.e., the benchmark of constant returns to scale in the CEO production function" (Gabaix and Landier 2006).

Figure 5.1   Share of foreign earnings in US corporate profits, 1970–2006

percent

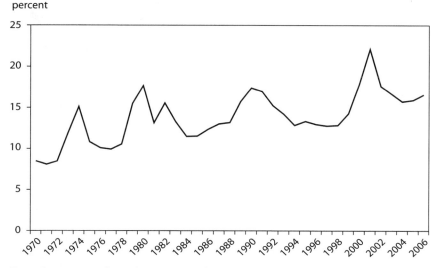

Note: Corporate profits with inventory valuation and capital consumption adjustments.
Source: US Bureau of Economic Analysis, National Income and Product Accounts, table 6.16, available at www.bea.gov.

of US multinational corporations accounted for 22 percent of total value-added by US multinational corporations (table 5.1). This share was almost the same as that two decades earlier.[14] Similarly, while 21 percent of all those employed by US multinational corporations worked in MOFAs in 1982, by 2000 the share had grown to only 25 percent.

While these data indicate that multinational firms have not become more globalized, it is likely that more US firms have become multinational. So to confirm my conclusion, I use a broader measure and consider the share of all US corporate earnings earned abroad. Using national income data, I find that although it increased after 2000, the share of US corporate profits from the rest of the world was basically the same in 2000 as it was in the early 1980s—around 15 percent (figure 5.1) and though higher on average after 2000 than earlier, in 2006 the share was actually lower than in 1990 or 1980.[15] To be sure, the size and value of US firms have increased

---

14. Bureau of Economic Analysis, Operations of US Multinational Companies, *Survey of Current Business,* July 2005.

15. The average share was 13.7 percent in the 1980s and 14.3 percent in the 1990s. These are derived from Bureau of Labor Statistics, US National Income Accounts, table 6.16.

16. However, between 2000 and 2005, the share of value-added in US parents did fall—from 78 to 73 percent.

because their overseas operations have grown, but the growth on account of these global operations has not been disproportionate to the initial share of overseas operations in 1980.[16] If CEO pay had been tied to stock market values, and these values related to firm output and/or profits, then the role played in pay increases by global activities would have simply been proportional to their 1980 share.

Other Top Earners

Dew-Becker and Gordon (2007) and Stephen N. Kaplan and Joshua Ruah (2007) present different views of the importance of CEOs in the incomes of the super rich. Kaplan and Ruah have made some headway in documenting who the other members of this select group are. In particular, they focus on four groups, which together account for about 10 percent of the top 0.5 percent of adjusted gross income (AGI). In addition to the top business executives, they consider financial executives, lawyers, and professional athletes and celebrities. They find that a remarkably small share—only about 2 percent of the top 0.5 percent of AGI—actually comes from those who work on "main street" as executives in the top nonfinancial corporations, with an equal number from lawyers in top Wall Street firms. A much larger number, about half of their sample, are financial executives, investment bankers, and asset managers and hedge fund operators. They add that individuals missing from their sample are likely to be trial lawyers, executives of privately held companies, highly paid doctors, and independently wealthy individuals who are hard to track down (Kaplan and Ruah 2007).

Dew-Becker and Gordon (2007) argue that the contributions of executives to wage inequality at the very top is more significant than their contribution to measures that include other sources of income. Nonetheless, all agree that top executives are not the whole of the story. The richest Americans actually come from a wide range of industries and occupations. According to tax returns, the top 1 percent of earners, for example, come from all across the economy and some are employed in sectors that are primarily domestic in orientation. They include business professionals such as lawyers and doctors, private entrepreneurs who own their own businesses, sports stars, movie producers and entertainers, and above all financiers. In 2004, only 14.2 percent of this top 1 percent is involved in tradable goods production—i.e., in agriculture, mining, and durable and nondurable goods (table 5.2).

The same logic that Gabaix and Landier use to explain the disproportionate increase in the earnings of the most talented executives can also be used to account for the explosive earnings of many of these other top 1 percent of wage earners. Indeed, the essential elements in the explanation were well recognized over 100 years ago by Alfred Marshall and formal-

Table 5.2   Percentage of taxpayers in the top 1 percent of earners, by sector, 2004

Sector	Percent
Finance, insurance, and real estate	13.2
Legal, accounting, and other professionals	9.2
Manufacturing: Durable goods	8.1
Education	6.9
Other medical	6.8
Business and repair	6.0
Retail trade	5.0
Construction	4.9
Hospitals	4.2
Wholesale trade	4.1
Manufacturing: Nondurable goods	3.2
Public administration (justice, public order, and safety)	3.0
Transportation	2.6
Agriculture	2.4
Communications	1.8
Entertainment	1.1
Utilities	1.1
Mining	0.5
No category	14.3

Source: Hodge and Moody (2004).

ized by Sherwin Rosen (1981). Marshall pointed out how particular patterns of demand and supply could create opportunities for earnings to become especially concentrated at the top of the income distribution:

> There never was a time at which moderately good oil paintings sold more cheaply than now, and there never was a time at which first-rate paintings sold so dearly. A business man of average ability and average good fortune gets now a lower rate of profits on his capital than at any previous time; while yet the operations, in which a man exceptionally favored by genius and good luck can take part, are so extensive as to enable him to amass a huge fortune with a rapidity hitherto unknown.
>
> The causes . . . are chiefly two; firstly, the general growth of wealth; and secondly, the development of new facilities for communication, by which men, who have once attained a commanding position, are enabled to apply their constructive or speculative genius to undertakings vaster, and extending over a wider area, than ever before.
>
> It is the first cause, almost alone, that enables some barristers to command very high fees; for a rich client whose reputation, or fortune, or both, are at stake will scarcely count any price too high to secure the services of the best man he can get: and it is this again that enables jockeys and painters and musicians of exceptional ability to get very high prices. In all these occupations the highest incomes earned in our own generation are the highest that the world has yet seen. (Marshall 1920, book VI, chapter XII, 41–43)

On the demand side, superstars emerge when buyers place a particular premium on paying for the very best. Whereas under normal circumstances, an increase in the price of a product leads consumers to purchase close substitutes, in these special cases, inferior goods and services are viewed as very poor substitutes. This could be true for the services of CEOs, but it could also be true of the demand for the services of top performers, professionals, and of course, athletes. But such demand patterns are not sufficient. For prices to be high, supplies of the highest quality services must not be able to keep pace with demand expansion. In some cases, this could be the case because what is being sought is "a positional good" or service (Hirsch 1976). By definition, only one lawyer can be "the best lawyer," only one runner can hold the world record, and only one plot of land can be located in the very center of the city. As the demand for the best increases, so too do the earnings of the best, and that is why increasingly there are forces for "the winner to take all."[17]

Winners could also become even wealthier if technological advances permit them to extend their supply at low cost to all those willing to buy. In this case, the superstars' incomes rise because of increased volumes rather than the prices of their services. These real superstars will typically emerge when the services they provide, like public goods, can be provided at low marginal cost to a large number of consumers. On the supply side, a key issue is thus the ability of the producers to replicate their services at sufficient quality on a sufficient scale.

Just after the paragraphs quoted above, Marshall pointed out that the earnings of even the very best singers in his day were limited by the capacity of the theatres in which they sang:

> So long as the number of persons who can be reached by a human voice is strictly limited, it is not very likely that any singer will make an advance on the £10,000, said to have been earned in a season by Mrs Billington at the beginning of last century. (Marshall 1920, book VI, chapter XII, 43)

Marshall was, however, prescient about the importance of the development of communications. Today advances in information technology, which can, almost without additional cost, replicate the performances of the very best actors and musicians in film, video and audio cassettes, and compact discs, allow them to command increasingly large incomes. Technological developments that thus bias returns toward the very skilled are clearly an important part of this story.[18]

For the most part, therefore, the primary drivers of the increased returns of the super rich are their ability to appropriate rents from growing

---

17. See the superb discussion of these forces in Frank and Cook (1995).

18. Ironically, the circle seems to be turning. According to Krueger (2005), as music has increasingly been downloaded free, superstars have raised their concert prices because they are now less likely to boost their record sales.

Table 5.3   US parent share in US multinational value-added, 1999 and 2004 (percent)

Sector	1999	2004
All	77	73
Mining	51	63
Utilities	92	92
Manufacturing	71	64
Wholesale trade	73	78
Information	92	88
Motion picture	85	72
Broadcasting	93	87
Finance	81	82
Securities	83	83
Insurance	81	81
Professional services	71	69
Architecture and engineering	78	81
Computer systems	60	56
Management consulting	80	68
Advertising	67	74
Other	92	89
Other	88	85

Source: Mataloni and Yorgas (2006).

markets because of their relatively unique and specific abilities. These are not individuals whose incomes reflect the increased returns to widely possessed general skills. Indeed, an essential feature of the economics of superstars is precisely that they do not have close substitutes. It is likely, therefore, that these increased returns reflect developments in and are confined to quite narrow sectors and activities, many of which have nothing to do with international trade. Whereas increased demand for unskilled workers in one part of the economy could increase wages of unskilled workers throughout the economy, an increase in the demand for plastic surgeons will do little for the earnings of college graduates elsewhere or even other doctors.

The largest single group of these superstars operates in US financial markets. They have benefited from the dramatic increase in the size and scope of these markets over the past two decades. This increase has meant particularly large incomes when these result from fees tied to transactions. Just as entertainers benefit when their work can be replicated on a large scale, so do those in financial markets when a given amount of work can be spread over transactions with increasing scale. But again, surprisingly, the largest US firms in finance still reap the preponderance of their incomes from their domestic activity. The earnings of financial firms (securities and insurance, for example) are actually more concentrated in the

United States than those of multinational corporations as a whole. In 2004, 82 percent of the earnings of these firms were derived from their domestic activities (table 5.3). According to data in Kaplan and Ruah (2007, table 2A), with the exception of Credit Suisse First Boston, Citibank, and Goldman Sachs, most other major US financial firms earn almost 80 percent of their incomes in the United States.

It is likely, therefore, that the richest and most talented Americans do owe some of their success to their increased ability to sell in global markets, but it does not appear that, for the most part, their increased prosperity is very heavily linked to trade.[19] Larger and freer global markets due to digitization, technological improvements in communications, deregulation, and liberalization do give more scope for higher incomes for entertainers and sports stars, filmmakers, and producers of products with large upfront costs, such as software. It is also true that as a result of globalization, there are increased opportunities for traders, private equity, hedge funds, and others who operate and invest in international financial markets. But there are more important technological and institutional forces operating in the domestic economy that are providing opportunities for "winners" to do particularly well.

Many of the highest US earners have benefited from strong US equity markets, since they are paid in the form of (nonqualified) stock options that count as wage incomes when exercised, while others have made killings as venture capitalists in initial public offerings. But again, the booming domestic economy in the late 1990s was the strongest force driving the stock market. Similarly, the soaring pay of some successful professionals and proprietors may have an international component, but many have made their money in successful purely domestically oriented businesses and professions. While globalization's marginal contribution is impossible to quantify, a reasonable statement would be that globalization is not a disproportionately important source of the recent gains of the top US wage earners.

---

19. To some degree, trade agreements have played a role. The increased enforcement of intellectual property protection made possible by the World Trade Organization has contributed to the enhanced profitability of innovations in pharmaceuticals, audio-visual productions, and information technology—particularly in some developing countries that had not provided such protection until recently.

6

Job Dislocation: Past and Future

This study has focused on wages and inequality, but when it comes to trade another major concern for all workers—particularly for blue-collar workers—relates to job dislocation. The US labor market is in a constant state of change, with a large number of jobs continuously being created and destroyed. In 2005, for example, private-sector employment expanded by 2.1 million jobs. But this *net* increase was achieved by gross employment changes, which at the establishment level were of a bigger magnitude: 31.4 million jobs were created to offset 29.3 million jobs that were destroyed.[1] Most of these changes took place because existing establishments expanded or contracted, but beyond these changes, 5.8 million jobs were destroyed due to existing establishments closing and 6.2 million were created due to new establishments opening.

Not all of this destruction is unwanted, however. The worker-establishment data from the Bureau of Labor Statistics show that more than half of the separations are voluntary "quits" rather than involuntary layoffs and discharges, but nonetheless many workers still lose their jobs for reasons beyond their direct control. In three years from January 2003 to December 2005, for example, even though total employment increased by 4.7 million, 8.1 million workers (or 6.1 percent of all workers) could be classified as displaced. Of these, 3.8 million had held their jobs for more than three years.[2]

---

1. The establishment-level data are from the Bureau of Labor Statistics, Business Employment Dynamics database, and the worker-establishment data are from the Bureau of Labor Statistics, Job Openings and Labor Turnover Survey.

2. Displaced workers are defined as persons 20 years of age and older who lost or left jobs because their plant or company closed or moved, there was insufficient work for them to do,

Similarly, despite the strong job market, in 2005, 1.8 million workers were subject to mass layoffs, in which more than 50 workers were laid off from a single establishment.[3] Similarly, in 2005, although manufacturing employment in the aggregate remained roughly constant, 670,000 workers were subject to mass layoffs.[4]

Considerable evidence indicates that such involuntary job loss can be costly. Research on displacement from manufacturing in general and from import-competing industries in particular has found that about two-thirds of displaced workers find new full-time jobs—but at an average wage loss of 17 percent if one accounts for forgone wage growth during the unemployment transition. This average disguises a range of experiences: Thirty-six percent gained reemployment at or above previous earnings, whereas 25 percent suffered earnings losses of 30 percent or more.[5]

What explains this range of reemployment outcomes is not the cause of dislocation. Indeed, the experiences of workers displaced from industries heavily affected by trade are generally quite similar to those of workers displaced from other manufacturing activities, for example. The business cycle is an important influence on the costs of displacement. Adjustments are more painful during recessions, when job losses are more common and more concentrated. Mass layoffs, for example, averaged 2.5 million in the recession year of 2001 but only 1.5 million in 2006. But beyond business cycles, the characteristics of workers themselves are very important determinants of reemployment outcomes.

Lori Kletzer (2001) reports that more-educated workers are less likely to lose their jobs, more likely to change jobs with less cost, and less likely to suffer declines in reemployment earnings. In contrast, the largest declines in reemployment earnings tend to be realized by workers who are older, less-skilled, and with established tenure. This central role for skills in understanding job transitions shows up in broader measures such as unemployment rates: In 2007, for example, the US unemployment rate for high-school dropouts was 7.2 percent, in contrast to just 1.8 percent for college graduates.

Given the magnitude of job transitions and the costs of involuntary displacement, workers are understandably concerned about employment se-

or their position or shift was abolished. Between January 2001 and December 2003, total employment fell by 2.1 million, and 11.4 million workers experienced such displacement (US Census Bureau and Bureau of Labor Statistics, Current Population Survey, Worker Displacement, 2003–2005, available at www.bls.gov).

3. Data are from the Bureau of Labor Statistics, Mass Layoff Statistics, available at www.bls.gov/mls.

4. Even though between 2000 and 2006 it accounted for 13 percent of total employment between 2000 and 2006, manufacturing accounted for 40 percent of all mass layoffs over the same period.

5. These data are from Kletzer (2001). The 17 percent is from Farber (2005).

curity. Indeed, in the United States, worker surveys indicate that insecurity has been rising: Despite the long economic expansion of the 1990s, US workers in the 1990s reported feeling more pessimistic about losing their jobs than in the 1980s (Schmidt 1999). And there is evidence that the expansion of international trade and investment in particular may raise worker insecurity. Workers in the United Kingdom employed in sectors with high levels of foreign investment are much more likely to report greater economic insecurity (Scheve and Slaughter 2004). And US workers in service activities and occupations that are potentially tradable report both greater insecurity and a stronger desire for a strong government safety net (Anderson and Gascon 2007).

Are these concerns warranted? Are globally engaged firms and industries likely to be less stable than those that are not? Economic theory gives some reason to expect greater instability. Just as globalization increases consumer choice, it also increases the options firms have in their production decisions. With the option of participating in global production networks or sourcing from abroad, firms can be more responsive to costs of all kinds—wage costs included. This greater cost sensitivity can result in more-volatile employment outcomes for workers.[6]

The empirical evidence on global engagement and employment instability remains somewhat mixed. Early research on US manufacturing plants, for example, found that most job creation and destruction was from idiosyncratic plant-specific shocks rather than from broader forces such as regional or industry wages or trade flows (Davis, Haltiwanger, and Schuh 1996). Of course, plant-specific shocks may themselves have been the result of global engagement: This speaks to an important limitation of much of the data that researchers use to try to disentangle the myriad influences of globalization and other forces. Recent work on services, in contrast, finds that jobs in occupations and industries in services that are potentially tradable (both domestically and internationally) have recently been less secure. For example, from 2001 to 2003 job loss rates for displaced workers were 12.8 percent for those working in tradable services versus just 7.3 percent for those in nontradable services (Jensen and Kletzer 2005).

Beyond the long-standing issues about job destruction and dislocations, the 2001 recession and subsequent recovery have added new concerns about the costs of global engagement.

---

6. Technically, as Dani Rodrik (1997) emphasizes the demand curve for labor becomes more elastic so that given shifts have a greater employment impact. Matthew J. Slaughter (2001) does find evidence that US labor demand for production (but not nonproduction) workers became more elastic over time but states that the hypothesis that trade contributed to this growing elasticity "receives mixed support at best." Similarly, Pravin Krishna, Mitra Devashish, and Sajjid Chinoy (2002) find no increases in labor demand elasticity in Turkey.

New Concerns about Job Dislocation from Global Engagement

Manufacturing

One new feature has been the sharp and sustained drop in US manufacturing employment, a sector that historically has employed a disproportionate share of blue-collar workers, particularly men. While remaining fairly constant over the 1990s, total employment in US manufacturing fell sharply around the 2001 recession, from 17.3 million in mid-2000 to just 14.3 million by the end of 2003. Employment then drifted down even further, to just 14.1 million in 2007.

Domestic factors, in particular the combination of slow growth in demand, especially the investment slump, and rapid growth in productivity, have been the dominant source of the job loss. But US trade performance—in particular, very weak export growth—played a significant role as well. The share of manufacturing job loss between 2000 and 2003 that can be attributed to trade has been estimated at somewhere between 12 percent (Baily and Lawrence 2004) and 33 percent (Bivens 2004, 2006): a minority, yes, but one that few would deny has been both significant and persistent.[7]

More-Educated Workers

Second, in the 2001 recession, the share of more-educated workers rendered unemployed increased. Estimates show that in 2003, 9.9 percent of all workers with a college degree or higher had been displaced during the past three years: the highest such share ever recorded. This displacement may have reflected the secular rise in educational attainment of the overall labor force but may also have reflected features particular to this recession (such as the concentration of employment declines in manufacturing just discussed).

Reemployment

Third, following the 2001 recession, a sizable share of the unemployed has found it difficult to secure reemployment. Long unemployment spells can be particularly painful for many reasons: for example, after six months when unemployment benefits typically expire. Recent unemployment rates of 4.5 to 5 percent have historically been associated with average

---

7. From 2003 and 2005, import growth was a source of the failure of manufacturing employment to grow.

unemployment spells of about 12 weeks and long-term unemployment shares of 11 percent. In the current recovery, however, average unemployment spells have been 18 weeks, and the long-term unemployment share has averaged over 18 percent (Mishel, Bernstein, and Allegretto 2007).

Services Offshoring

The fourth and perhaps most important new concern about job dislocation from global engagement relates to the spread of offshoring of services activities. Anecdotes now abound in the business media that, thanks to the information technology (IT) revolution in recent years—in particular, the spread around the globe of the internet—many workers across the skills spectrum now face competition from overseas outsourcing in traditionally nontraded activities such as business services and programming.[8] When juxtaposed with the recent persistent unemployment spells and relatively high dislocations of more skilled workers, these anecdotes have contributed to a widespread perception that global engagement in services is now destroying new swatches of American jobs.

Although such services outsourcing is indeed growing rapidly, to date it remains too small in scale to account for ongoing patterns of US job destruction. For example, in the years of slow US employment growth from 2001 through 2004, total employment in India of business process outsourcing services grew by about 400,000—only some of which was devoted to servicing the US market.[9] Several studies confirm that thus far, offshoring has been quite limited.[10] Indeed, the limited role played by offshoring of all kinds in layoffs is apparent in recent Bureau of Labor Statistics surveys.[11]

The bigger and still-open question is the future breadth and impact of services offshoring in particular. Former Vice Chairman of the US Federal Reserve Alan Blinder has argued that IT-enabled services offshoring is likely to be a major source of job disruption in the future, particularly for relatively educated US workers, who have generally believed their jobs to be insulated from international competition. Blinder (2007) has calculated

---

8. See the particularly interesting account of one such exaggeration in Levy and Yu (2006). See also National Academy of Public Administration (2006a, 2006b).

9. Data from India's National Association of Software and Service Companies (NASSCOM), quoted in Baily and Lawrence (2004, note 24).

10. See National Academy of Administration (2006a, 2006b), Amiti and Wei (2005), and IMF (2007), all of which find that while it has grown in recent years, offshoring of services remains very limited.

11. In 2004 of almost 1 million jobs lost in extended mass layoffs only 73,217 were found to be due to outsourcing. Of that 7 out of 10 of cases that could be verified, were to domestic outsourcing and 3 out of 10 to offshoring. See Brown and Siegel (2005).

a "mid-range" estimate that 26 percent of all US jobs could be potentially exposed to international competition from trade in general and offshoring in particular.

How large is this estimate? Roughly 12 percent of Americans currently work in manufacturing, mining, and agriculture, and about another 3 or 4 percent in services exports. These numbers mean that Blinder's estimates imply that an additional 10 percent of the labor force could potentially face direct competition via global engagement. This figure is a large increase, but it would still mean that the majority of American jobs would not face such direct competition. It should also be stressed that this figure may be an overestimate since it is based on technological possibilities that do not directly account for the many other barriers (legal, cultural, and regulatory) that could inhibit such movements even when the outsourcing technology might work. And however large the spread of services offshoring turns out to be, this transition is likely to unfold over many years if not decades.

Juxtaposed against the current churn of US jobs described above, this degree of adjustment, particularly when it occurs over a long period of time, does not seem very large. And indeed, if Blinder's estimate is correct, as it undergoes this offshoring adjustment, the US labor market, rather than going into unchartered waters, would be returning to a level of international exposure it has already experienced. In 1970, for example, the share of Americans employed in manufacturing, mining, and agriculture was 26 percent—the same share that could be exposed according to Blinder's estimate of potential offshorability.

Are Borders Irrelevant?

The crucial question is, how quickly are these changes likely to occur? My answer based on the evidence from the goods market is that change will come slowly. Thomas L. Friedman's book *The World Is Flat* (2005) notwithstanding, an overwhelming amount of empirical evidence indicates that the world is actually round (and bumpy).[12] To be sure, trade *is* affected by relative prices and costs, but borders continue to matter a lot, and adjustments across borders are very slow. The full effects of exchange rates on trade flows, for example, can take up to five years. The many gravity models that have been estimated confirm that distance is important and by an amount that is much greater than can be ascribed to transportation costs. Similarly, detailed comparisons of price differentials in Bradford and Lawrence (2004), for example, show that absolute price differences of similar goods have averaged 20 percent between the United States and

---

12. For a superb and entertaining review of Friedman's book (2005) that makes similar points, see Leamer (2007).

Canada, 30 percent between the United States and Europe, and 50 percent between the United States and Japan, and yet still are not arbitraged away.

Why? Even when communication and transportation costs are zero, a large number of obstacles and inhibitions remain: These include differences in laws, culture, language, policies, regulations, and standards. Moreover, it is not enough just to know that a service can be obtained more cheaply. Particularly for complex transactions that require depending on foreign suppliers for key inputs, old relationships must be broken and new ones established. And building the necessary trust will require time and favorable experiences. And on the supply side, Indians and others have to build their capacity and skills and establish their reputations. The implication is that on both the demand and supply sides, adjustments are bound to be protracted.

Nonetheless, declining natural barriers to global engagement, thanks to IT, is expanding the cross-border opportunities for many previously nontradable service activities. And these expanding pressures of global engagement will undoubtedly reach many highly skilled Americans, not just their lower-skilled counterparts.

Trade has contributed to the decline in manufacturing employment in the United States, thereby reducing job opportunities for less skilled blue-collar workers, but this decline is predominantly a reflection of relatively faster productivity growth in the sector. Moreover, simulation estimates in Baily and Lawrence (2004) suggest that even if the United States is successful in bringing the large current account into balance, the additional employment that is created is unlikely to prevent further declines in the share of US employment in the manufacturing sector.

In sum, the US system is in a constant state of change because of a large number of factors. International trade is one of the factors causing the dislocation of American workers, but it is considerably less important than the business cycle, technology, productivity growth, and competition between domestic firms. Education is important in limiting the costs and reducing the incidence of dislocation, but it is no panacea. Accordingly, the challenge for policy is helping workers undertake these adjustments, regardless of their source.

7

Conclusion

Over the past quarter century, increasing inequality of three types explain in part the gap between the real wages of blue-collar workers and the rise in output per worker. But they don't tell the full story. Indeed, about 60 percent of the shortfall in the gap can be explained by nonwage benefits and the price measures used to deflate wages and output, and an additional 10 percent reflects the relatively greater improvements in white-collar skills and education. Nonetheless, about 30 percent of the gap does reflect the fact that others have earned a larger piece of the income pie.

The rise in the wage premiums skilled workers earned in the 1980s and 1990s is widely known and recognized. Even though the causes of the increase remain in dispute, technological change is widely seen as the major reason, with most studies suggesting that trade was responsible for about 20 percent of the rise. The most surprising conclusion of this study, however, is that the recent increase in US inequality has little to do with global forces that might be expected to especially affect unskilled workers—namely, immigration and expanded trade with developing countries. Indeed, between 2000 and 2006, most relative wage measures show little change. Instead, the sources of increased inequality have been the rising share of the super rich—a development in which trade is likely to have played only a small role—and the increased share of profits in income, much of which could be cyclical.

While increased trade has made some contributions, both to wage and super rich inequality, it should be acknowledged that trade is just one of many sources of structural change in the US economy, and isolating its particular contribution to both inequality and displacement is difficult. The US economy is in a continuous state of flux, buffeted by technological and institutional innovations, demographic changes, cyclical fluctuations, government policy changes, and many other powerful factors that shape the competitive struggles between firms.

Because all these forces shape labor-market outcomes, and because most of these would be present even if the US economy were isolated from the rest of the world, the key policy challenge is not trying to isolate and limit the pressures of globalization or other changes but rather dealing directly with inequality and equipping American workers, firms, and communities to adapt to shocks of all kinds.[1]

There is overwhelming evidence that, on balance, increased global engagement benefits the United States and that additional liberalization could add to these gains. It can be conservatively stated that US GDP is 10 percent higher because of global engagement and that the benefits from liberalization vastly outweigh the costs even when adjustment costs are taken into account. It would be unfortunate, therefore, if the concerns about inequality and dislocation were used to halt that movement or to adopt new protectionist measures that are likely to be ineffective in dealing with these problems.

Moreover, America's integration into the world economy has been driven not just by falling barriers due to policy but also by falling natural barriers. In the past decade, for example, arguably the most important change in globalization has been the revolution in information technology, which has widened the range of service activities tradable across borders. Government trade policies would have almost no ability to thwart the flows that have been facilitated by these advances and other forms of falling natural trade barriers. Accordingly, many of globalization's pressures on Americans today would persist regardless of US trade policy.

A far better approach, therefore, would be to reap the gains from trade through additional liberalization and to deal with inequality directly through a more progressive tax system and with job dislocation through programs that assist workers in adapting to structural change regardless of its source.

---

1. For a complete program, see Aldonas, Lawrence, and Slaughter (2007).

Appendix A

Table A.1   Decomposition of the gap between output per hour and blue-collar wages, 1981–2006 (log points, 1981 = 0)

Year	bw/cpi (a)	bw/pbus (b)	bcomp/pbus (c)	eci/pbus (d)	comp/pbus (e)	composition (f)
1981	0	0	0	0	0	0
1982	0	0.3	1.1	1.4	1.4	1.0
1983	−0.2	1.0	3.2	3.6	2.2	1.4
1984	−0.4	1.6	4.6	5.8	3.5	1.5
1985	−0.1	2.9	5.8	7.6	6.0	1.8
1986	0.7	3.8	6.9	9.3	9.3	2.2
1987	0	4.4	7.4	10.4	10.9	2.5
1988	−0.4	4.5	8.7	11.6	12.7	3.3
1989	−1.2	4.2	8.9	12.6	11.7	3.7
1990	−2.4	4.3	9.9	13.8	14.3	4.2
1991	−2.7	4.5	10.9	14.9	15.9	5.4
1992	−2.5	5.3	12.8	16.8	19.1	6.6
1993	−2.3	5.9	14.5	18.3	19.2	6.8
1994	−1.5	7.0	15.7	19.8	18.9	7.3
1995	−1.0	8.2	16.4	20.7	19.3	7.4
1996	−0.7	9.5	17.4	22.0	21.2	7.8
1997	0.3	11.2	18.4	23.6	22.8	8.5
1998	2.0	13.7	20.5	26.3	28.1	8.7
1999	3.2	16.0	22.5	28.7	31.9	9.4
2000	3.6	17.8	24.9	31.3	36.8	9.4
2001	4.6	19.7	26.7	33.7	39.0	10.2
2002	5.9	21.6	29.2	36.1	41.4	11.3
2003	6.0	22.6	31.8	38.5	43.8	11.8
2004	5.3	22.5	33.6	39.7	45.8	12.0
2005	4.9	22.0	33.6	39.9	46.5	12.1
2006	4.9	22.6	34.5	41.3	48.6	12.4

bw = blue-collar wages from employment cost index (ECI)
bcomp = blue-collar compensation from ECI
comp = business-sector hourly compensation
composition = Bureau of Labor Statistics multifactor productivity growth estimate of labor force
   composition
cpi = consumer price index
eci = employment cost index
output/hour = business-sector output per hour of all persons
pbus = business-sector implicit price deflator

output/hour (g)	Prices (h) (b – a)	Benefits (i) (c – b)	Wage inequality (j) (d – c)	Skills (k) .75 × (f – j)	Super rich inequality (l) e – (d + k)	Class inequality (profits) (m) (g – e)
0	0	0	0	0	0	0
−0.9	0.2	0.8	0.3	0.5	−0.4	−2.3
2.7	1.1	2.2	0.5	0.7	−2.1	0.4
5.3	1.9	3.1	1.2	0.3	−2.6	1.8
7.5	3.0	2.9	1.9	0	−1.6	1.5
10.6	3.1	3.1	2.4	−0.1	0	1.3
11.1	4.4	3.0	3.1	−0.4	0.9	0.2
12.7	4.9	4.3	2.9	0.3	0.8	−0.1
13.6	5.4	4.7	3.7	0	−0.9	2.0
15.7	6.7	5.6	3.8	0.3	0.2	1.4
17.1	7.2	6.4	4.0	1.0	0	1.2
21.3	7.8	7.5	4.0	2.0	0.3	2.2
21.7	8.2	8.6	3.8	2.3	−1.4	2.5
22.8	8.5	8.7	4.1	2.5	−3.3	3.9
22.9	9.2	8.3	4.3	2.4	−3.8	3.6
25.9	10.2	7.8	4.7	2.4	−3.3	4.8
27.8	10.9	7.3	5.1	2.5	−3.3	5.0
30.6	11.6	6.8	5.9	2.1	−0.3	2.5
33.5	12.8	6.6	6.1	2.4	0.8	1.5
36.2	14.3	7.1	6.4	2.2	3.3	−0.6
38.7	15.1	7.0	7.0	2.4	3.0	−0.3
42.7	15.7	7.6	6.9	3.4	1.9	1.3
46.5	16.6	9.2	6.7	3.9	1.5	2.6
49.8	17.2	11.2	6.1	4.5	1.6	4.1
51.6	17.1	11.6	6.3	4.3	2.3	5.1
53.3	17.7	11.9	6.8	4.2	3.1	4.7

References

Abowd, John, and Michael Bognonno. 1995. International Differences in Executive and Managerial Compensation. In *Differences and Changes in Wage Structures*, ed. Richard B. Freeman and Lawrence F. Katz. National Bureau of Economic Research, Comparative Labor Markets Series. Chicago: University of Chicago Press.

Aldonas, Grant D, Robert Z. Lawrence, and Matthew J. Slaughter. 2007. *Succeeding in the Global Economy: A New Policy Agenda for the American Worker.* Washington: Financial Services Forum.

Alesina, Alberto, and Edward Glaeser. 2004. *Fighting Poverty in the US and Europe: A World of Difference.* Oxford: Oxford University Press.

Amiti, Mary, and Shang-Jin Wei. 2005. Fear of Service Outsourcing: Is It Justified? *Economic Policy* 20 (April): 308–47.

Anderson, Richard G., and Charles S. Gascon. 2007. *The Perils of Globalization: Offshoring and Economic Insecurity of the American Worker.* Federal Reserve Bank of St. Louis Working Paper 2007-004A. St. Louis, MO: Federal Reserve Bank of St. Louis.

Autor, David H., Lawrence F. Katz, and Melissa S. Kearney. 2005. *Trends in U.S. Wage Inequality: Re-Assessing the Revisionists.* NBER Working Paper 11627. Cambridge, MA: National Bureau of Economic Research.

Autor, David H., Lawrence F. Katz, and Melissa S. Kearney. 2006. *The Polarization of the U.S. Labor Market.* NBER Working Paper 11986. Cambridge, MA: National Bureau of Economic Research.

Baicker, Katherine, and Amitabh Chandra. 2006. The Labor Market Effects of Rising Health Insurance Premiums. *Journal of Labor Economics* 24, no. 3: 609–34.

Baily, Martin N., and Robert Z. Lawrence. 2004. What Happened to the Great U.S. Job Machine? The Role of Trade and Electronic Offshoring. *Brookings Papers on Economic Activity 2004*, no. 2. Washington: Brookings Institution.

Baldwin, Robert E., and Glen G. Cain. 1997. *Shifts in U.S. Relative Wages: The Role of Trade, Technology, and Factor Endowments.* NBER Working Paper 5934. Cambridge, MA: National Bureau of Economic Research.

Bebchuk, Lucian A., and Jesse M. Fried. 2003. Executive Compensation as an Agency Problem. *Journal of Economic Perspectives* 17, no. 3 (summer): 71–92.

Bebchuk, Lucian A., and Yaniv Grinstein. 2005. *The Growth of Executive Pay.* NBER Working Paper 11443. Cambridge, MA: National Bureau of Economic Research.

Bernard, Andrew, J. Bradford Jensen, and Peter K. Schott. 2006. Survival of the Best Fit: Competition from Low-Wage Countries and the (Uneven) Growth of U.S. Manufacturing Firms. *Journal of International Economics* 68, no. 1 (January): 219–37.

Bhagwati, Jagdish. 1991. *Free Traders and Free Immigrationists: Strangers or Friends?* Russell Sage Foundation Working Paper. New York: Russell Sage Foundation.

Bivens, Josh L. 2004. *Shifting Blame for Manufacturing Job Loss: Effect of Rising Trade Deficit Shouldn't Be Ignored.* Economic Policy Institute Briefing Paper 149. Washington: Economic Policy Institute.

Bivens, Josh L. 2006. *Trade Deficits and Manufacturing Job Loss: Correlation and Causality.* Economic Policy Institute Briefing Paper 171. Washington: Economic Policy Institute.

Blanchard, Olivier J. 1998. *Revisiting European Unemployment: Employment, Capital Accumulation, and Factor Prices.* NBER Working Paper 6566. Cambridge, MA: National Bureau of Economic Research.

Bloom, Nicholas, and John Van Reenen. 2007 (forthcoming). Measuring and Explaining Management Practices Across Firms and Countries. *Quarterly Journal of Economics* CXXII.

Blinder, Alan S. 2006. Offshoring: The Next Industrial Revolution? *Foreign Affairs* 85, no. 2 (March–April): 113–28.

Blinder, Alan S. 2007. Off-shoring: Big Deal or Business as Usual? Paper presented at the Alvin Hansen Seminar at Harvard University, May 2.

Borjas, George J. 2003. Comments in *Inequality in America: What Role for Human Capital Policies?* by James J. Heckman and Alan B. Krueger. Cambridge, MA: MIT Press.

Borjas, George J., Richard B. Freeman, and Lawrence F. Katz. 1997. How Much Do Immigration and Trade Affect Labor Market Outcomes? *Brookings Papers on Economic Activity* 1997, no. 1: 1–90. Washington: Brookings Institution.

Bosworth, Barry, and George L. Perry. 1994. Productivity and Real Wages: Is There a Puzzle? *Brookings Papers on Economic Activity 1994*, no. 1: 317–43. Washington: Brookings Institution.

Bradford, Scott C., and Robert Z. Lawrence. 2004. *Has Globalization Gone Far Enough? The Costs of Fragmented Markets.* Washington: Institute for International Economics.

Bradford, Scott C., Paul L. E. Grieco, and Gary Clyde Hufbauer. 2005. The Payoff to America from Global Integration. In *The United States and the World Economy: Foreign Economic Policy for the Next Decade,* by C. Fred Bergsten and the Institute for International Economics. Washington: Institute for International Economics.

Brown, Sharon P., and Lewis B. Siegel. 2005. Mass Layoff Data Indicate Outsourcing and Offshoring Work. *Monthly Labor Review* (August): 3–10.

Card, David, and John E. DiNardo. 2002. Skill-Biased Technological Change and Rising Wage Inequality: Some Problems and Puzzles. *Journal of Labor Economics* 20, no. 4: 733–83.

CBO (Congressional Budget Office). 2007. *Changes in the Economic Resources of Low-Income Households with Children.* Washington (May).

Cline, William R. 1997. *Trade and Income Distribution.* Washington: Institute for International Economics.

Conyon, Martin, and Kevin Murphy. 2000. The Prince and the Pauper? CEO Pay in the United States and the United Kingdom. *Economic Journal* CX: 640–71.

Davis, Steven J., John C. Haltiwanger, and Scott Schuh. 1996. *Job Creation and Destruction.* Cambridge, MA: MIT Press.

Deardorff, Alan V., and Dalia S. Hakura. 1994. Trade and Wages: What Are the Questions? In *Trade and Wages: Leveling Wages Down?* ed. Jagdish Bhagwati and Marvin Kosters. Washington: American Enterprise Institute.

Deardorff Alan V., and Robert W. Staiger. 1988. An Interpretation of the Factor Content of Trade. *Journal of International Economics* 24, no. 1/2 (February): 93–107.

Dew-Becker, Ian, and Robert J. Gordon. 2005. Where Did Productivity Growth Go? Inflation Dynamics and the Distribution of Income. *Brookings Papers on Economic Activity 2005,* no. 2: 67–150. Washington: Brookings Institution.

Dew-Becker, Ian, and Robert J. Gordon. 2007 (forthcoming). Unresolved Issues in the Rise of American Inequality. *Brookings Papers on Economic Activity.* Washington: Brookings Institution.

Farber, Henry S. 2005. *What Do We Know about Job Loss in the United States? Evidence from the Displaced Workers Survey, 1984–2004.* Princeton University Working Paper 498. Princeton, NJ: Industrial Relations Section, Princeton University.

Feenstra, Robert C. 2004. *Advanced International Trade: Theory and Evidence.* Princeton, NJ: Princeton University Press.

Feenstra Robert C., and Gordon H. Hanson. 1999. The Impact of Outsourcing and High-Technology Capital on Wages: Estimates for the United States, 1979–1990. *Quarterly Journal of Economics* 114: 907–40.

Frank, Robert H., and Philip J. Cook. 1995. *The Winner-Takes-All Society.* New York: The Free Press.

Friedman, Thomas L. 2005. *The World Is Flat: A Brief History of the Twenty-First Century.* New York: Farrar, Straus, Giroux.

Frydman, Carola, and Raven E. Saks. 2007. Executive Compensation: A New View from a Long-Term Perspective. MIT Sloan School, Cambridge, MA. Photocopy.

Gabaix, Xavier, and Augustin Landier. 2006. Why Has CEO Pay Increased So Much? NBER Working Paper 12365. Cambridge, MA: National Bureau of Economic Research. (Forthcoming in the *Quarterly Journal of Economics.*)

Glaeser, Edward L. 2005. *Inequality.* Harvard Institute of Economic Research Discussion Paper 2078 (July). Cambridge, MA: Harvard University.

Goldin, Claudia, and Lawrence Katz. 2007 (forthcoming). Long-Run Changes in the U.S. Wage Structure: Narrowing, Widening, Polarizing. *Brookings Papers on Economic Activity.* Washington: Brookings Institution.

Gottschalk, Peter, and Sheldon Danziger. 2003. Wage Inequality, Earnings Inequality and Poverty in the U.S. Over the Last Quarter of the Twentieth Century. Boston College Working Paper 560. Chestnut Hill, MA: Boston College.

Guscina, Anastasia. 2007. *Effects of Globalization on Labor's Share in National Income.* IMF Working Paper 06/294 (January). Washington: International Monetary Fund.

Hall, Brian J., and Jeffrey B. Liebman. 1998. Are CEOs Really Paid Like Bureaucrats? *Quarterly Journal of Economics* 113 (August): 653–91.

Hall, Brian, and Kevin J. Murphy. 2003. The Trouble with Stock Options. *Journal of Economic Perspectives* 17, no. 3 (Summer): 51.

Harrigan, James. 2000. International Trade and American Wages in General Equilibrium 1967–1995. In *The Impact of International Trade on Wages,* ed. Robert C. Feenstra. National Bureau of Economic Research Conference Report. Chicago: University of Chicago Press.

Harrison, Anne E. 2002. Has Globalization Eroded Labor's Share? Some Cross-Country Evidence. University of California at Berkeley. Photocopy.

Hirsch, Fred. 1976. *Social Limits to Growth.* Cambridge, MA: Harvard University Press.

Hodge, Scott, and J. Scott Moody. 2004. *Wealthy Americans and Business Activity.* Tax Foundation Special Report 131 (August). Washington: Tax Foundation.

IMF (International Monetary Fund). 2007. World Economic Outlook: Spillovers and Cycles in the Global Economy. In *The Globalization of Labor.* Washington (April).

Jensen, J. Bradford, and Lori Kletzer. 2005. *Tradable Services: Understanding the Scope and Impact of Services Outsourcing.* Institute for International Economics Working Paper 05-9. Washington: Institute for International Economics.

Jensen, Michael C., and Kevin J. Murphy. 1990. Performance Pay and Top-Management Incentives. *Journal of Political Economy* 98, no. 2 (April): 225–64.

Kaplan, Steven N., and Joshua Rauh. 2007. Wall Street and Main Street: What Contributes to the Rise in the Highest Incomes? University of Chicago Business School. Photocopy (July).

Kletzer, Lori, G. 2001. *Job Loss from Imports: Measuring the Costs.* Washington: Institute for International Economics.

Krishna, Pravin, Mitra Devashish, and Sajjid Chinoy. 2002. Trade Liberalization and Labor-Demand Elasticities: Evidence from Turkey. *Journal of International Economics* 55: 391–409.

Krueger, Alan B. 1997. *Labor Market Shifts and the Price Puzzle Revisited.* NBER Working Paper 5924. Cambridge, MA: National Bureau of Economic Research.

Krueger, Alan B. 2005. The Economics of Real Superstars: The Market for Rock Concerts in the Material World. *Journal of Labor Economics* 23, no. 1.

Krugman, Paul R. 1995. Growing World Trade: Causes and Consequences. *Brookings Papers on Economic Activity 1995*, no. 1: 327–77.

Krugman, Paul R. 2007. *Trade and Inequality Revisited.* Vox (June 15). Available at www. voxeu.org.

Krugman, Paul R., and Maurice Obstfeld. 2000. *International Economics: Theory and Policy.* Boston: Addison Wesley.

Lardy, Nicholas R. 2005. China: The Great New Economic Challenge? In *The United States and the World Economy: Foreign Economic Policy for the Next Decade,* by C. Fred Bergsten and the Institute for International Economics. Washington: Institute for International Economics.

Lawrence, Robert Z. 1996. *Single World, Divided Nations.* Washington: Brookings Institution.

Lawrence, Robert Z., and Matthew L. Slaughter. 1993. Trade and US Wages in the 1980s: Giant Sucking Sound or Small Hiccup? *Brookings Papers on Economic Activity: Microeconomics 1993*, no. 2: 161–210. Washington: Brookings Institution.

Leamer, Edward E. 1998. In Search of Stolper-Samuelson Linkages Between International Trade and Lower Wages. In *Imports, Exports, and the American Worker,* ed. Susan Collins. Washington: Brookings Institution.

Leamer, Edward E. 2007. A Flat World: A Level Playing Field, A Small World after All, or None of the Above? A Review of Thomas L. Friedman's *The World Is Flat. Journal of Economic Literature* (March) XLV, no. 1: 83–126.

Lemieux, Thomas. 2006. Increasing Residual Wage Inequality: Composition Effects, Noisy Data and Rising Demand for Skill? *American Economic Review* 96, no. 3 (June): 461–98.

Levy, Frank, and Peter Temin. 2007. *Inequality and Institutions in 20th Century America.* MIT Department of Economics Working Paper 07-17 (May 1). Cambridge, MA: Massachusetts Institute of Technology.

Levy, Frank, and Kyoung-Hee Yu. 2006. *Offshoring of Professional Services: Radiology Services from India.* MIT Industrial Performance Center Working Paper MIT-IPC-06-005 (March). Cambridge, MA: Massachusetts Institute of Technology.

Llg, Randy E. 2006. Change in Employment by Occupation, Industry and Earnings Quartile, 2000–05. *Monthly Labor Review* (December): 21–34.

Mann, Catherine L., with Jacob Funk Kirkegaard. 2006. *Accelerating the Globalization of America: The Role for Information Technology.* Washington: Institute for International Economics.

Marshall, Alfred. 1920. *Principles of Economics.* Macmillan and Co., Ltd.

Mataloni, Raymond J., and Daniel R. Yorgas. 2006. Operations of Multinational Companies. *Survey of Current Business* (November). Washington: Bureau of Economic Analysis, US Department of Commerce.

Mishel, Lawrence, and Jared Bernstein. 1998. Technology and the Wage Structure: Has Technology's Impact Accelerated since the 1970s? *Research in Labor Economics* 17.

Mishel, Lawrence, Jared Bernstein, and Sylvia Allegretto. 2007. *The State of Working America 2006/2007.* Washington and Ithaca, NY: Economic Policy Institute and Cornell University Press.

National Academy of Public Administration. 2006a. *Off-shoring: An Elusive Phenomenon.* Academy Project no. 2051-000 (January). Washington.

National Academy of Public Administration. 2006b. *Off-shoring: How Big Is IT?* Academy Project no. 2051-000 (October). Washington.

Pierce, Brooks. 2001. Compensation Inequality. *Quarterly Journal of Economics* 116, no. 4 (November): 1493–525.

Reynolds, Alan. 2007. *Has US Income Inequality Really Increased?* Cato Institute Policy Analysis 586 (January). Washington: Cato Institute.

Roach, Stephen S. 2006. *From Globalization to Localization*. Morgan Stanley Research Global (December 14). New York: Morgan Stanley.

Rodrik, Dani. 1997. *Has Globalization Gone Too Far?* Washington: Institute for International Economics.

Rodrik, Dani. 2006. *What's So Special About China's Exports?* NBER Working Paper 11947. Cambridge, MA: National Bureau of Economic Research.

Rose, Stephen. 2007. *Does Productivity Growth Still Benefit Working Americans? Unravelling the Income Growth Mystery to Determine How Much Median Incomes Trail Productivity Growth.* Washington: The Information Technology and Innovation Foundation (June).

Rosen, Sherwin. 1981. The Economics of Superstars. *American Economic Review* 71 (December): 845–58.

Ruser, John W. 2001. The Employment Cost Index: What Is It? *Monthly Labor Review* (September).

Sachs, Jeffrey D., and Howard Shatz. 1994. Trade and Jobs in U.S. Manufacturing. *Brookings Papers on Economic Activity 1994*, no. 1: 1–84. Washington: Brookings Institution.

Samuelson, Paul A. 1948. International Trade and the Equalization of Factor Prices. *Economic Journal* 58, no. 230 (June): 163–84.

Scheve, Kenneth F., and Matthew J. Slaughter. 2004. Economic Insecurity and the Globalization of Production. *American Journal of Political Science* 48, no. 4.

Schmidt, Stefanie R. 1999. Long-Run Trends in Workers' Beliefs about Their Own Job Security: Evidence from the General Social Survey. *Journal of Labor Economics* 17, no. 4: S127–S141.

Schott, Peter K. 2004. Across Product Versus Within-Product Specialization in International Trade. *Quarterly Journal of Economics* 119, no. 2 (May): 647–78.

Schumacher Dirk, Jan Hatzius, and Tetsufumi Yamakawa. 2007. Rising Income Inequality in the G3. *Global Economics Paper* 158 (July). New York: Goldman Sachs.

Shelburne, Robert C. 2004. Trade and Inequality: The Role of Vertical Specialization and Outsourcing. *Global Economy Journal* 4, no. 2, article 2.

Slaughter, Matthew J. 2000. What Are the Results of Product-Price Studies? In *The Impact of International Trade on Wages*, ed. Robert C. Feenstra. National Bureau of Economic Research Conference Report. Chicago: University of Chicago Press.

Slaughter, Matthew J. 2001. International Trade and Labor-Demand Elasticities. *Journal of International Economics* 54, no. 1: 27–56.

Slaughter, Matthew J., and Kenneth F. Scheve. 2007. A New Deal for Globalization. *Foreign Affairs* 86, no. 4 (July/August): 34–48.

Stolper, Wolfgang, and Paul A. Samuelson. 1941. Protection and Real Wages. *Review of Economic Studies* 9, no. 1 (November): 58–73.

Summers, Lawrence H. 1989. Some Simple Economics of Mandated Benefits. *American Economic Review* 79: 177–83.

Schwink, Albert E. 1997. Differences Among Private Industry Occupational Groups in Pay Levels and Trends. *Compensation and Working Conditions* (Winter): 13–19. Washington: Bureau of Labor Statistics.

Wood, Adrian. 1994. *North-South Trade, Employment and Inequality: Changing Fortunes in a Skill-Driven World.* Oxford: Clarendon Press.

Wood, Adrian. 1995. How Trade Hurt Unskilled Workers. *Journal of Economic Perspectives* 9, no. 3 (Summer): 57–80.

Yellen, Janet L. 2006. Economic Inequality in the United States. Speech to the Center for the Study of Democracy University of California, Irvine, November 6.

Index

compensation
CEO (*See* chief executive officer [CEO] compensation)
deflators, 18–19
measurement of, 21
performance-based, full deduction of, 56
share in national income, 23*n*, 47–52, 48*t*, 48*n*–49*n*, 49*f*
total, benefits included in, 17*f*, 17–18
compensation by industry data (ECI), 30, 30*t*
compensation inequality, versus wage inequality, 18*n*
competition
effect of trade on, 5*n*, 11
international, adaptation to, 38–39, 43, 45
consumer price index, 18
consumption concept, versus production concept, 18
corporate profits. *See* profits
cultural differences, job dislocation and, 71
Current Population Survey (CPS), 16, 22

deflators, 18–19
demand
labor, 67*n*
super rich inequality and, 61–62
developing countries
imports from, 25–26, 31–33, 32*f*, 73
prices and, 33*f*, 33–34, 34*f*
wage income and, 5–7, 9–12, 37–38, 43–44
production processes in, 39, 43
dollar devaluations, 31

earnings. *See* compensation; income; wage income
econometric techniques, 36
Economic Policy Institute, 42
education. *See also* college-educated workers
job displacement and, 66, 68, 71
productivity and, 19
wage income and, 37, 37*f*
Employer Costs for Employee Compensation (ECEC), 20*n*
employment cost index (ECI), 15, 15*n*
blue-collar compensation, 17*f*, 18–19, 27
blue-collar wage series, 4*f*, 15–17, 17*f*
class inequality and, 47

compensation by industry, 30, 30*t*
occupational compensation series, 28, 29*t*, 30
super rich inequality and, 53–54

factor intensity reversals, absence of, 38–39
factors of production, 25–26
mobility of, 26*n*, 26–27
financial executives, 60–64
firm size. *See also* multinational corporations
CEO compensation and, 57–58, 58*n*
foreign direct investment, 4–5

GDP, share of trade in, 31–32, 32*f*, 74
globalization, 11, 74
adaptation to, 38–39, 43, 45
job dislocation and, 70–71
public opinion of, 6, 30
super rich inequality and, 12, 24, 53–64
trends in, 48–49
wage growth and, 4–10, 46
goods industries
import growth, 31–34, 32*f*, 33*f*
labor compensation in, 30, 30*t*

health care benefits, 51
Hecksher-Ohlin model, 25–26
hourly compensation, 21
hourly earnings distribution by industry, 39–40, 40*t*

immigration, 45, 73
import(s)
composition, 31–33, 32*f*
from developing countries, wage income and, 5–7, 9–12, 37–38, 43–44
price data, 33*f*, 33–34, 34*f*
import displacement, 11–12, 39
income. *See also* compensation; wage income
effect of taxes and transfers on, 9
social factors affecting, 9, 9*n*
versus wealth, 8
income inequality
explanations for, 3–4, 8, 73–74
measurement of, 8–10
policy response to, 13, 74
versus poverty, 7–8
public opinion of, 47
types of, 7, 73
inequality. *See specific type of inequality*

Other Publications from the Peterson Institute

International Debt Reexamined*
William R. Cline
February 1995   ISBN 0-88132-083-8
American Trade Politics, 3d ed.
I. M. Destler
April 1995   ISBN 0-88132-215-6
Managing Official Export Credits:
The Quest for a Global Regime*
John E. Ray
July 1995   ISBN 0-88132-207-5
Asia Pacific Fusion: Japan's Role in APEC*
Yoichi Funabashi
October 1995   ISBN 0-88132-224-5
Korea-United States Cooperation in the New
World Order* C. Fred Bergsten and Il SaKong, eds.
February 1996   ISBN 0-88132-226-1
Why Exports Really Matter!* ISBN 0-88132-221-0
Why Exports Matter More!* ISBN 0-88132-229-6
J. David Richardson and Karin Rindal
July 1995; February 1996
Global Corporations and National Governments
Edward M. Graham
May 1996   ISBN 0-88132-111-7
Global Economic Leadership and the Group of
Seven   C. Fred Bergsten and C. Randall Henning
May 1996   ISBN 0-88132-218-0
The Trading System after the Uruguay Round*
John Whalley and Colleen Hamilton
July 1996   ISBN 0-88132-131-1
Private Capital Flows to Emerging Markets
after the Mexican Crisis*
Guillermo A. Calvo, Morris Goldstein,
and Eduard Hochreiter
September 1996   ISBN 0-88132-232-6
The Crawling Band as an Exchange Rate Regime:
Lessons from Chile, Colombia, and Israel
John Williamson
September 1996   ISBN 0-88132-231-8
Flying High: Liberalizing Civil Aviation
in the Asia Pacific*
Gary Clyde Hufbauer and Christopher Findlay
November 1996   ISBN 0-88132-227-X
Measuring the Costs of Visible Protection
in Korea*   Namdoo Kim
November 1996   ISBN 0-88132-236-9
The World Trading System: Challenges Ahead
Jeffrey J. Schott
December 1996   ISBN 0-88132-235-0
Has Globalization Gone Too Far?
Dani Rodrik
March 1997   ISBN paper 0-88132-241-5
Korea-United States Economic Relationship*
C. Fred Bergsten and Il SaKong, editors
March 1997   ISBN 0-88132-240-7
Summitry in the Americas: A Progress Report
Richard E. Feinberg
April 1997   ISBN 0-88132-242-3
Corruption and the Global Economy
Kimberly Ann Elliott
June 1997   ISBN 0-88132-233-4

Regional Trading Blocs in the World
Economic System   Jeffrey A. Frankel
October 1997   ISBN 0-88132-202-4
Sustaining the Asia Pacific Miracle:
Environmental Protection and Economic
Integration   Andre Dua and Daniel C. Esty
October 1997   ISBN 0-88132-250-4
Trade and Income Distribution
William R. Cline
November 1997   ISBN 0-88132-216-4
Global Competition Policy
Edward M. Graham and J. David Richardson
December 1997   ISBN 0-88132-166-4
Unfinished Business: Telecommunications
after the Uruguay Round
Gary Clyde Hufbauer and Erika Wada
December 1997   ISBN 0-88132-257-1
Financial Services Liberalization in the WTO
Wendy Dobson and Pierre Jacquet
June 1998   ISBN 0-88132-254-7
Restoring Japan's Economic Growth
Adam S. Posen
September 1998   ISBN 0-88132-262-8
Measuring the Costs of Protection in China
Zhang Shuguang, Zhang Yansheng,
and Wan Zhongxin
November 1998   ISBN 0-88132-247-4
Foreign Direct Investment and Development:
The New Policy Agenda for Developing
Countries and Economies in Transition
Theodore H. Moran
December 1998   ISBN 0-88132-258-X
Behind the Open Door: Foreign Enterprises
in the Chinese Marketplace   Daniel H. Rosen
January 1999   ISBN 0-88132-263-6
Toward A New International Financial
Architecture: A Practical Post-Asia Agenda
Barry Eichengreen
February 1999   ISBN 0-88132-270-9
Is the U.S. Trade Deficit Sustainable?
Catherine L. Mann
September 1999   ISBN 0-88132-265-2
Safeguarding Prosperity in a Global Financial
System: The Future International Financial
Architecture, Independent Task Force Report
Sponsored by the Council on Foreign Relations
Morris Goldstein, Project Director
October 1999   ISBN 0-88132-287-3
Avoiding the Apocalypse: The Future
of the Two Koreas   Marcus Noland
June 2000   ISBN 0-88132-278-4
Assessing Financial Vulnerability: An Early
Warning System for Emerging Markets
Morris Goldstein, Graciela Kaminsky,
and Carmen Reinhart
June 2000   ISBN 0-88132-237-7
Global Electronic Commerce: A Policy Primer
Catherine L. Mann, Sue E. Eckert,
and Sarah Cleeland Knight
July 2000   ISBN 0-88132-274-1

WORKS IN PROGRESS

DISTRIBUTORS OUTSIDE THE UNITED STATES

**Australia, New Zealand,
and Papua New Guinea**
D. A. Information Services
648 Whitehorse Road
Mitcham, Victoria 3132, Australia
Tel: 61-3-9210-7777
Fax: 61-3-9210-7788
Email: service@dadirect.com.au
www.dadirect.com.au

India, Bangladesh, Nepal, and Sri Lanka
Viva Books Private Limited
Mr. Vinod Vasishtha
4737/23 Ansari Road
Daryaganj, New Delhi 110002
India
Tel: 91-11-4224-2200
Fax: 91-11-4224-2240
Email: viva@vivagroupindia.net
www.vivagroupindia.com

**Mexico, Central America, South America,
and Puerto Rico**
US PubRep, Inc.
311 Dean Drive
Rockville, MD 20851
Tel: 301-838-9276
Fax: 301-838-9278
Email: c.falk@ieee.org

Asia (*Brunei, Burma, Cambodia, China,
Hong Kong, Indonesia, Korea, Laos, Malaysia,
Philippines, Singapore, Taiwan, Thailand,
and Vietnam*)
East-West Export Books (EWEB)
University of Hawaii Press
2840 Kolowalu Street
Honolulu, Hawaii 96822-1888
Tel: 808-956-8830
Fax: 808-988-6052
Email: eweb@hawaii.edu

Canada
Renouf Bookstore
5369 Canotek Road, Unit 1
Ottawa, Ontario K1J 9J3, Canada
Tel: 613-745-2665
Fax: 613-745-7660
www.renoufbooks.com

Japan
United Publishers Services Ltd.
1-32-5, Higashi-shinagawa
Shinagawa-ku, Tokyo 140-0002
Japan
Tel: 81-3-5479-7251
Fax: 81-3-5479-7307
Email: purchasing@ups.co.jp
*For trade accounts only. Individuals will find
Institute books in leading Tokyo bookstores.*

Middle East
MERIC
2 Bahgat Ali Street, El Masry Towers
Tower D, Apt. 24
Zamalek, Cairo
Egypt
Tel. 20-2-7633824
Fax: 20-2-7369355
Email: mahmoud_fouda@mericonline.com
www.mericonline.com

United Kingdom, Europe
(*including Russia and Turkey*), **Africa,
and Israel**
The Eurospan Group
c/o Turpin Distribution
Pegasus Drive
Stratton Business Park
Biggleswade, Bedfordshire
SG18 8TQ
United Kingdom
Tel: 44 (0) 1767-604972
Fax: 44 (0) 1767-601640
Email: eurospan@turpin-distribution.com
www.eurospangroup.com/bookstore

Visit our website at:
www.petersoninstitute.org
E-mail orders to:
petersonmail@presswarehouse.com